Questions
of Life

By the same author:
Why Jesus?
Why Christmas?
Searching Issues
A Life Worth Living
Telling Others
Challenging Lifestyle
30 Days
The Heart of Revival

See pages 263-264 for more information.

Nicky Gumbel

Questions of Life

A Practical Introduction to the Christian Faith

Cook Ministry Resources, a division of Cook Communications Ministries
Colorado Springs, Colorado / Paris, Ontario

Cook Ministry Resources is a division of Cook Communications Ministries International (CCMI). In fulfilling its mission to encourage the acceptance of Jesus Christ as personal Savior and to contribute to the teaching and putting into practice of His two great commandments, CCMI creates and disseminates Christian communication materials and services to people throughout the world.

Questions of Life
by Nicky Gumbel
Copyright © Nicky Gumbel 1993, 1996

Published by Cook Communications Ministries. All rights reserved in North America.

This edition issued by special arrangement with Kingsway Publications, Lottbridge Drove, Eastbourne, East Sussex, England BN23 6NT. The right of Nicky Gumbel to be identified as author of this work has been asserted by him in accordance with the Copyright, Designs and Patents Act 1988.

First published 1993
This edition first published 1996

Study Guide © David Stone 1995
Illustrations by Charlie Mackesy
Design by Blum Graphic Design

Unless otherwise indicated, biblical quotations are from the New International Version © 1973, 1978, 1984 by the International Bible Society, used by permission of Zondervan Bible Publishers.

ISBN 0-7814-5261-9

10 11 12 13 14 Printing/Year 05 04 03 02

Contents

Foreword

This book has come at exactly the right time. It fills a gap that has existed in Christian literature for several years. On the one hand, as recent well-documented figures show, the church has been losing members at an alarming rate—more than half a million over the last ten years in England alone. During the same time, major denominations in North America have also seen a significant decline in church membership and attendance. Even more significantly, eighty percent of people leaving the church are under the age of twenty. While it is certainly true that a number of churches are showing very encouraging signs of growth, the overall picture is still one of perceived dullness, decay, and, as Nicky shows in this book, disillusion generally with church life. And yet, there is beyond any question a very considerable new interest in spiritual things, together with a hunger and growing hope that somewhere, somehow, there may be found a contemporary answer to the age-old question, "What is truth?"

Questions of Life is a sympathetic, fascinating, and immensely readable introduction to Jesus Christ—still the most attractive and captivating person possible to know. Nicky Gumbel's intelligent, well researched, and informed approach ensures that the search for Truth fully engages our minds as well as our hearts.

I am very glad that all the hard work that Nicky has put into the *Alpha Course* here, through which thousands of people have been deeply affected, is now available to an even wider public. I have no hesitation in highly commending this readable and important book.

Sandy Millar
Holy Trinity Brompton

Preface

There is today a new interest in the Christian faith, and more specifically in the person of Jesus. Nearly two thousand years since His birth, He has approaching two billion followers. Christians will always be fascinated by the founder of their faith and the Lord of their lives. But now, there is a resurgence of interest among non-churchgoers. Many are asking questions about Jesus. Was He merely a man, or is He the Son of God? If He is, what are the implications for our everyday lives?

This book attempts to answer some of the key questions at the heart of the Christian faith. It is based on *"Alpha,"* a course started at Holy Trinity Brompton in London for non-churchgoers, those seeking to find out more about Christianity, and those who have recently come to faith in Jesus Christ. It has been running for several years and has grown substantially. Thousands of men and women of all ages have come to the course full of questions about Christianity, and have found God as their Father, Jesus Christ as their Savior and Lord, and the Holy Spirit as the One who comes to live within them.

I would like to thank all the people who have read and offered constructive criticisms on the manuscripts, and Cressida Inglis-Jones who typed the original manuscript and almost all the revisions with great speed, efficiency, and patience.

Nicky Gumbel

1 Christianity: Boring, Untrue, and Irrelevant?

For many years I had three objections to the Christian faith. First, I thought it was boring. I went to chapel at school and found it very dull. I felt sympathy with Robert Louis Stevenson who once entered in his diary, as if recording an extraordinary phenomenon, "I have been to Church today, and am not depressed." In a similar vein, the American humorist Oliver Wendell Holmes wrote, "I might have entered the ministry if certain clergymen I knew had not looked and acted so much like undertakers." My impression of the Christian faith was that it was dreary and uninspiring.

Secondly, it seemed to me to be untrue. I had intellectual objections to the Christian faith and, rather pretentiously, I called myself a logical determinist. When I was fourteen I wrote an essay in which I tried to destroy the whole of Christianity and disprove the existence of God. Rather surprisingly, it was nominated for a prize! I had knock-down arguments against the Christian faith and rather enjoyed arguing with Christians, thinking I had won some great victory.

Thirdly, I thought that Christianity was irrelevant. I could not see how something that happened two thousand years ago and two thousand miles away in the Middle East could have any relevance to my life in twentieth-century Britain. We often used to sing that much-loved hymn "Jerusalem" which asks, "And did those feet in ancient time walk upon England's mountains green?" We all knew that the answer was, "No, they did not." It seemed to be totally irrelevant to my life.

I realize, with hindsight, that it was partly my fault, because I never really listened and was totally ignorant about the Christian

Men and women were created to live in a relationship with God.

faith. Many people today, in our secularized society, don't know much about Jesus Christ or what He did, or anything to do with Christianity. One hospital chaplain listed some of

the replies he was given to the question, "Would you like Holy Communion?" These are some of the answers:

- "No thanks, I'm Church of England."
- "No thanks, I asked for Cornflakes."
- "No thanks, I've never been circumcised."[1]

Christianity is far from boring, it is not untrue and it is not irrelevant. On the contrary, it is exciting, true, and relevant. Jesus said, "I am the way and the truth and the life" (John 14:6). If He was right, and I believe He was, then there can be nothing more important in this life than our response to Him.

DIRECTION FOR A LOST WORLD

Men and women were created to live in a relationship with God. Without that relationship there will always be a hunger, an emptiness, a feeling that something is missing. Prince Charles once spoke of his belief that, for all the advances of science, "there remains deep in the soul (if I dare use that word), a persistent and unconscious anxiety that something is missing, some ingredient that makes life worth living."

Bernard Levin, perhaps the greatest English columnist of this generation, once wrote an article called "Life's Great Riddle, and No Time to Find Its Meaning." In it he spoke of the fact that in spite of his great success as a columnist for over twenty years, he feared that he might have "wasted reality in the chase of a dream." He wrote:

> To put it bluntly, have I time to discover why I was born before I die? ... I have not managed to answer the question yet, and however many years I have before me they are certainly not as many as there are behind. There is an obvious danger in leaving it too late ... why do *I have* to know why I was born? Because, of course, I am unable to believe that it was an accident; and if it wasn't one, it must have a meaning.[2]

Levin is not a Christian and wrote emphatically, "For the fourteen thousandth time, I am not a Christian." Yet he seems to be only too aware of inadequate answers to the meaning of life. He wrote:

> Countries like ours are full of people who have all the material comforts they desire, together with such non-material blessings as a happy family, and yet lead lives of quiet, and at times noisy, desperation, understanding nothing but the fact that there is a hole

inside them and that however much food and drink they pour into it, however many motor cars and television sets they stuff it with, however many well balanced children and loyal friends they parade around the edges of it ... it aches.[3]

Some people spend much of their lives seeking something that will give meaning and purpose to life. Leo Tolstoy, author of *War and Peace*, wrote a book called *A Confession* in 1879 in which he tells the story of his search for meaning and purpose in life. He had rejected Christianity as a child. When he left the university he sought to get as much pleasure out of life as he could. He entered the social world of Moscow and St. Petersburg, drinking heavily, living promiscuously, gambling, and leading a wild life. But it did not satisfy him.

Then he became ambitious for money. He had inherited an estate and made a large amount of money out of his books. Yet that did not satisfy him either. He sought success, fame, and importance. These he also achieved. He wrote what the *Encyclopedia Britannica* describes as "one of the two or three greatest novels in world literature." But he was left asking the question, "Well fine ... so what?" to which he had no answers.

He was left asking, "Well fine ... so what?" to which he had no answers.

Then he became ambitious for his family, to give them the best possible life. He married in 1862 and had a kind, loving wife and thirteen children (which, he said, distracted him from any search for the overall meaning of life). He had achieved all his ambitions and was surrounded by what appeared to be complete happiness. And yet one question brought him to the verge of suicide: "Is there any meaning in my life which will not be annihilated by the inevitability of death which awaits me?"

He searched for the answer in every field of science and

philosophy. The only answer he could find to the question "Why do I live?" was that "in the infinity of space and the infinity of time infinitely small particles mutate with infinite complexity."

As he looked around at his contemporaries he saw that people were not facing up to the first order questions of life ("Where did I come from?" "Where am I heading?" "Who am I?" "What is life about?"). Eventually he found that the peasant people of Russia had been able to answer these questions

"Where did I come from? Where am I heading? Who am I? What is life about?"

through their Christian faith, and he came to realize that only in Jesus Christ do we find the answer.

Over a hundred years later nothing has changed. Freddie Mercury, the lead singer of the British rock group Queen, who died at the end of 1991, wrote in one of his last songs on *The Miracle* album, "Does anybody know what we are living for?" In spite of the fact that he had amassed a huge fortune and had attracted thousands of fans, he admitted in an interview shortly before his death that he was desperately lonely. He said, "You can have everything in the world and still be the loneliest man, and that is the most bitter type of loneliness. Success has brought me world idolization and millions of pounds, but it's prevented me from having the one thing we all need—a loving, ongoing relationship."

He was right to speak of an "ongoing relationship" as the one thing we all need. Yet no human relationship will satisfy entirely. Nor can it be completely ongoing. There always remains something missing. That is because we were created to live in a relationship with God. Jesus said, "I am the way." He is the only One who can bring us into that relationship with God that goes on into eternity.

When I was a child our family had an old black-and-white television set. We could never get a very good picture; it was always fuzzy and used to lose its horizontal hold. We were quite happy with it, since we did not know anything different. One day, we discovered that it needed an outside antenna! Suddenly we found that we could get clear and distinct pictures. Our enjoyment was transformed. Life without a relationship with God through Jesus Christ is like the television without the antenna.

 Life without a relationship with God is like a television without the antenna.

Some people seem quite happy, because they don't realize that there is something better. Once we have experienced a relationship with God, the purpose and meaning of life should become clear. We see things that we have never seen, and it would be foolish to want to return to the old life. We understand why we were made.

REALITY IN A CONFUSED WORLD

Sometimes people say, "It does not matter what you believe so long as you are sincere." But it is possible to be sincerely wrong. Adolf Hitler was sincerely wrong. His beliefs destroyed the lives of millions of people. The Yorkshire Ripper believed that he was doing God's will when he killed prostitutes. He, too, was sincerely wrong. His beliefs affected his behavior. These are extreme examples, but they make the point that it matters a great deal what we believe, because what we believe will dictate how we live.

Other people's response to a Christian may be, "It's great for you, but it is not for me." This is not a logical position. If Christianity is true, it is of vital importance to every one of us. If it is not true, Christians are deluded and it is not great for us—it is very sad, and the sooner we are put right the better. As the writer and scholar C. S. Lewis put it, "Christianity is a statement which, if false, is of *no* importance, and, if true, of infinite importance. The one thing it cannot be is moderately important."[4]

16

Is it true? Is there any evidence? Jesus said, "I am ... the truth." Is there any evidence to support His claim? These are some of the questions that we will be looking at later in the book. The linchpin of Christianity is the resurrection of Jesus Christ, and for that there is ample evidence. Professor Thomas Arnold, who as the headmaster of Rugby School revolutionized the concept of English education, was appointed to the chair of modern history at Oxford University. He was certainly a man well acquainted with the value of evidence in determining historical facts, and he said:

> I have been used for many years to studying the histories of other times, and to examining and weighing the evidence of those who have written about them, and I know of no one fact in the history of mankind which is proved by better and fuller evidence of every sort, to the understanding of a fair inquirer, than the great sign which God has given us that Christ died and rose again from the dead.

As we shall see later in the book, there is a great deal of evidence that Christianity is true. Yet, when Jesus said, "I am ... the truth," He meant more than intellectual truth. The original word for truth carries with it the notion of doing or experiencing the truth. There is something more to Christianity than an intellectual acceptance of the truth, and that is the knowledge of Jesus Christ who is *the* truth.

Suppose that before I met my wife, Pippa, I had read a book about her. Then, after I had finished reading the book I thought, "This sounds like a wonderful woman. This is the person I want to marry." There would be a big difference in my state of mind then— intellectually convinced that she was a wonderful person—and my state of mind now, after the experience of many years of marriage from which I can say, "I know she is a wonderful person." When a Christian says, in relation to his faith, "I know Jesus *is* the truth," he does not mean only that he knows intellectually that He is the truth, but that he has experienced Jesus *as* the truth. As we come into relationship with the One who is the truth, our perceptions change, and we begin to understand the truth about the world around us.

LIFE IN A DARK WORLD

Jesus said, "I am ... the life." In Jesus we find life where previously there has been guilt, addiction, fear, and the prospect of death. It is true that all of us were created in the image of God and there is, therefore, something noble about all human beings. However, we are all also fallen; we are born with a propensity to do evil. In every human being the image of God has been to a greater or lesser extent tarnished, and in some cases almost eradicated, by sin. Good and bad, strength and weakness coexist in all human beings. Aleksandr Solzhenitsyn, the Russian writer, said, "The line separating good and evil passes, not through states, nor through classes, nor between political parties ... but right through every human heart and through all human hearts."

I used to think I was a nice person because I didn't rob banks or commit other serious crimes. Only when I began to see my life alongside the life of Jesus Christ did I realize how much there was wrong. Many others have had this same experience. C. S. Lewis wrote: "For the first time I examined myself with a seriously practical purpose. And there I found what appalled me; a zoo of lusts, a bedlam of ambitions, a nursery of fears, a harem of fondled hatreds. My name was Legion."[5]

> I used to think I was a nice person because I didn't rob banks.

We all need forgiveness, and only in Christ can it be found. Marghanita Laski, the humanist, debating on television with a Christian, made an amazing confession. She said, "What I envy most about you Christians is your forgiveness." Then she added, rather pathetically, "I have no one to forgive me."

What Jesus did when He was crucified for us was to pay the penalty for all the things that we have done wrong. We will look at this subject in Chapter 3 in more detail. We will see that He died to remove our guilt, to set us free from addiction, fear, and ultimately death. He died instead of us.

On July 31, 1991 a remarkable event was celebrated. On the last day of July 1941, the Auschwitz sirens announced the escape of a prisoner. As a reprisal, ten of his fellow prisoners would die of a long, slow starvation, buried alive in a specially constructed, concrete bunker.

So all day, tortured by sun, hunger, and fear, the men waited as the German commandant and his Gestapo assistant walked between the ranks to select, quite arbitrarily, the chosen ten. As the commandant pointed to one man, Francis Gajowniczek, he cried out in despair, "My poor wife and children." At that moment the unimpressive figure of a man with sunken eyes and round glasses in wire frames stepped out of line and took off his cap. "What does this Polish pig want?" asked the commandant.

"I am a Catholic priest; I want to die for that man. I am old, he has a wife and children ... I have no one," said Father Maximilian Kolbe.

"Accepted," retorted the commandant, and moved on.

That night, ten men, including the priest, went to the starvation bunker. Normally they would tear each other apart like cannibals. Not so this time. While they had strength, lying naked on the floor, the men prayed and sang hymns. After two weeks, three of the men and Father Maximilian Kolbe were still alive. The bunker was required for others, so on August 14 the remaining four were disposed of. At 12:50 P.M., after two weeks in the starvation bunker and still conscious, the Polish priest was finally given an injection of phenol and died at the age of forty-seven.

He died to remove our guilt, to set us free. He died instead of us.

On October 10, 1982 in St. Peter's Square in Rome, Father Maximilian Kolbe's death was put in its proper perspective. Present in the crowd of 150,000 was Francis Gajowniczek, his wife, his children, and his children's children. Indeed, many had been saved by that one man. The Pope described Father Maximilian Kolbe's death: "This was victory won over all the systems of contempt and hate in man—a victory like that won by our Lord Jesus Christ."[6]

Jesus' death was, indeed, even more amazing because Jesus died, not just for one man, but for every single individual in the world. If you or I had been the only person in the world, Jesus Christ would have died instead of us to remove our guilt. When our guilt is removed, we have a new life.

Jesus not only died for us, He also rose again from the dead for us. In this act He defeated death. Most rational people are aware of the inevitability of death, although today some people make bizarre attempts to avoid it. The *Church of England Newspaper* described one such attempt:

In 1960 Californian millionaire James McGill died. He left detailed instructions that his body should be preserved and frozen in the hope that one day scientists might discover a cure for the disease that killed him. There are hundreds of people in Southern California who have put hopes of one day living again in this process which freezes and preserves human bodies. The latest development in Cryonics technology is called neuro-suspension which preserves just the human head. One reason why it is becoming popular is that it is much cheaper than preserving and maintaining a whole body. It reminds me of Woody Allen in *Sleeper*, where he preserved his nose.[7]

Such attempts to avoid the inevitability of death are plainly absurd and, indeed, unnecessary. Jesus came to bring us eternal life. Eternal life is a quality of life that comes from living in a relationship with God and Jesus Christ (John 17:3). Jesus never promised anyone an easy life, but He promised fullness of life (John 10:10). This new quality of life starts now and goes on into eternity. Our time on earth is relatively short, but eternity is vast. Through Jesus, who said, "I am ... the life," we can not only enjoy fullness of life here, but we can be sure that it will never end.

Christianity is not boring; it is about living life to the full. It is not untrue; it is *the* truth. It is not irrelevant; it transforms the whole of our lives. The theologian and philosopher Paul Tillich described the human condition as one that always involves three fears: fear about meaninglessness, fear about death, and fear about guilt. Jesus Christ meets each of these fears head on. He is vital to every one of us because He is "the way, and the truth, and the life."

2 Who is Jesus?

A missionary working among children in the Middle East was driving her jeep down a road when she ran out of gas. She had no gas can in her car. All she could find was a potty chair. She walked a mile down the road to the nearest gas station and filled the pot with gas. As she was pouring the gas into the tank of her jeep, a large Cadillac occupied by wealthy oil sheikhs drew up. They were absolutely fascinated at seeing her pouring the contents of the pot into the jeep. One of them opened the window and said, "My friend and I, although we do not share your religion, we greatly admire your faith!"

Some people see becoming a Christian as a blind leap of faith—the type of faith that would be needed in expecting a car to run on the usual contents of a potty chair. There is indeed a step of faith required. However, it is not a blind leap of faith, but a step of faith based on firm historical evidence. In this chapter I want to examine some of that historical evidence.

I am told that in a communist Russian dictionary Jesus is described as "a mythical figure who never existed." No serious historian could maintain that position today. There is a great deal of evidence for Jesus' existence. This comes not only from the Gospels and other Christian writings, but also from non-Christian sources. For example, the Roman historians Tacitus (directly) and Suetonius (indirectly) both write about Him. The Jewish historian Josephus, born in 37 A.D., describes Jesus and His followers thus:

Now there was about this time, Jesus, a wise man, if it be lawful to call him a man, for he was a doer of wonderful works, a teacher of such men as receive the truth with pleasure. He drew over to him both many of the Jews, and many of the Gentiles. He was [the] Christ; and when Pilate, at the suggestion of the principal men amongst us, had condemned him to the cross, those that loved him at first did not forsake him, for he appeared to them alive again the third day, as the divine prophets had foretold these and ten thousand other wonderful things concerning him; and the tribe of Christians so named after him, are not extinct at this day.[8]

So there is evidence outside the New Testament for the existence of Jesus. Furthermore, the evidence in the New Testament is very strong. Sometimes people say, "The New Testament was written a long time ago. How do we know that what they wrote down has not been changed over the years?" The answer is that we do know, very accurately through the science of

How do we know that what they wrote down has not been changed?

textual criticism, what the New Testament writers wrote. Essentially, the more texts we have, the less doubt there is about the original. The late Professor F. F. Bruce (who was Rylands professor of biblical criticism and exegesis at the University of Manchester) shows in his book *Are the New Testament Documents Reliable?* how rich the New Testament is in manuscript attestation by comparing the texts with other historical works.

The table on the next page summarizes the facts and shows the extent of the New Testament evidence.

Work	When Written	Earliest Copies	Time Span (yrs)	No. of copies
Herodotus	488-428 b.c.	900 a.d.	1,300	8
Thucydides	c. 460-400 b.c.	c. 900 a.d.	1,300	8
Tacitus	100 a.d.	1100 a.d.	1,000	20
Caesar's Gallic War	58-50 b.c.	900 a.d.	950	9-10
Livy's Roman History	59 b.c.–17 a.d.	900 a.d.	900	20
New Testament	40-100 a.d.	130 a.d. (full manuscripts 350 a.d.)	300	5,000 + Greek 10,000 Latin 9,300 others

F. F. Bruce points out that for Caesar's *Gallic War* we have nine or ten copies, and the oldest was written some nine hundred years later than Caesar's day. For Livy's *Roman History* we have not more than twenty copies, the earliest of which comes from around 900 A.D. Of the fourteen books of the histories of Tacitus, only twenty copies survive. Of the sixteen books of his *Annals*, ten portions of his two great historical works depend entirely on two manuscripts, one from the ninth century and one from the eleventh century. The history of

Thucydides is known almost entirely from eight manuscripts from about 900 A.D. The same is true of the history of Herodotus. Yet no classical scholar doubts the authenticity of these works, in spite of the large time gap and the relatively few manuscripts.

As regards the New Testament we have a great wealth of material. The New Testament was probably written between 40 and 100 A.D. We have excellent full manuscripts of the whole New Testament dating from as early as 350 A.D. (a time span of only three hundred years), papyri containing most of the New Testament writings dating from the third century, and even a fragment of John's Gospel dating from about 130 A.D. There are over five thousand Greek manuscripts, over ten thousand Latin manuscripts, and 9,300 other manuscripts, as well as over thirty-six thousand citings in the writings of the early church fathers. As one of the greatest textual critics ever, F. J. A. Hort, said, "In the variety and fullness of the evidence on which it rests, the text of the New Testament stands absolutely and unapproachably alone among ancient prose writings."9

> **"The New Testament stands absolutely and unapproachably alone …"**

F. F. Bruce summarizes the evidence by quoting Sir Frederic Kenyon, a leading scholar in this area:

> The interval then between the dates of original composition and the earliest extant evidence becomes so small as to be in fact negligible, and the last foundation for any doubt that the Scriptures have come down to us substantially as they were written has now been removed. Both the *authenticity* and the *general integrity* of the books of the New Testament may be regarded as finally established.10

We know from evidence outside and inside the New Testament

that Jesus existed.[11] But who is He? I heard Martin Scorsese say on television that he made the film *The Last Temptation of Christ* in order to show that Jesus was a real human being. Yet that is not the issue at the moment. Few people today would doubt that Jesus was fully human. He had a human body; He was sometimes tired (John 4:6) and hungry (Matthew 4:2). He had human emotions; He was angry (Mark 11:15-17), He loved (Mark 10:21), and He was sad (John 11:35). He had human experiences; He was tempted (Mark 1:13), He learned (Luke 2:52), He worked (Mark 6:3), and He obeyed His parents (Luke 2:51).

What many say today is that Jesus was *only* a human being—albeit a great religious teacher. The comedian Billy Connolly spoke for many when he said, "I can't believe in Christianity, but I think Jesus was a wonderful man."

What evidence is there to suggest that Jesus was more than just a wonderful man or a great moral teacher? The answer, as we shall see, is that there is a great deal of evidence. This evidence supports the Christian contention that Jesus was and is the unique Son of God. Indeed, He is God the Son, the second Person of the Trinity.

WHAT DID HE SAY ABOUT HIMSELF?

Some people say, "Jesus never claimed to be God." Indeed, it is true that Jesus did not go around saying the words, "I am God." Yet when one looks at all He taught and claimed, there is little doubt that He was conscious of being a man whose identity was God.

Teaching centered on Himself

One of the fascinating things about Jesus is that so much of His teaching was centered on Himself. He said to people, in effect, "If you want to have a relationship with God, you need to come to me" (see John 14:6). It's through a relationship with Him that we

27

encounter God.

The human heart has a deep hunger. The leading psychologists of the twentieth century have all recognized this. Freud said, "People are hungry for love." Jung said, "People are hungry for security." Adler said, "People are hungry for significance." Jesus said, "I am the bread of life" (John 6:35). In other words, "If you want your hunger satisfied, come to me."

Many people are walking in darkness, depression, disillusionment, and despair. They are looking for direction. Jesus said, "I am the light of the world. Whoever follows me will never walk in darkness, but will have the light of life" (John 8:12). Someone said to me after becoming a Christian, "It was as if the light had suddenly been turned on, and I could see things for the first time."

Many are fearful of death. One woman said to me that sometimes she couldn't sleep and that she would wake up in a cold sweat, fright-

ened about death, because she didn't know what was going to happen when she died. Jesus said, "I am the resurrection and the life. He who believes in me will live, even though he dies; and whoever lives and believes in me will never die" (John 11:25, 26).

So many are burdened by worries, anxieties, fears, and guilt. Jesus said, "Come to me, all you who are weary and burdened, and I will give you rest" (Matthew 11:28). They are not sure how to run their lives or who they should follow. I can remember that, before I was a Christian, I would be impressed by someone and want to be like that person, and then by a different person and follow that person. Jesus said, "Follow *me*" (Mark 1:17).

> **So many are burdened by worries, anxieties, fears, and guilt.**

He said to receive Him was to receive God (Matthew 10:40), to welcome Him was to welcome God (Mark 9:37), and to have seen Him was to have seen God (John 14:9). A child once drew a picture, and his mother asked what he was doing. The child said, "I am drawing a picture of God." The mother said, "Don't be silly. You can't draw a picture of God. No one knows what God looks like." The child replied, "Well, they will by the time I have finished!" Jesus said in effect, "If you want to know what God looks like, look at me."

Indirect claims

Jesus said a number of things which, although not direct claims to be God, show that He regarded Himself as being in the same position as God, as we will see in the examples that follow.

Authority to forgive sins. Jesus' claim to be able to forgive sins is well known. For example, on one occasion He said to a man who was paralyzed, "Son, your sins are forgiven" (Mark 2:5). The reaction of the religious leaders was, "Why does this fellow talk like that? He's blaspheming! Who can forgive sins but God alone?" Jesus went on to prove that He did have the authority to forgive sins by healing the paralyzed man. This claim to be able to forgive sins is indeed an astonishing claim.

C. S. Lewis puts it well when he says in his book *Mere Christianity*:

> One part of the claim tends to slip past us unnoticed because we have heard it so often that we no longer see what it amounts to. I mean the claim to forgive sins: any sins. Now unless the speaker is God, this is really so preposterous as to be comic. We can all understand how a man forgives offenses against himself. You tread on my toe and I forgive you, you steal my money and I forgive you. But what should we make of a man, himself unrobbed and untrodden on, who announced that he forgave you for treading on other men's toes and stealing other men's money? Asinine fatuity is the kindest description we should give of his conduct. Yet this is what Jesus did. He told people that their sins were forgiven, and never waited to consult all the other people whom their sins had undoubtedly injured. He unhesitatingly behaved as if He was the party chiefly concerned, the person chiefly offended in all offenses. This makes sense only if He really was the God whose laws are broken and whose love is wounded in every sin. In the mouth of any speaker who is not God, these words would imply what I can only regard as a silliness and conceit unrivaled by any other character in history.[12]

Judge of the world. Another extraordinary claim that Jesus made was that one day He would judge the world (Matthew 25:31-32). He

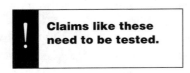

Claims like these need to be tested.

said He would return and "sit on his throne in heavenly glory" (vs. 31). All the nations would be gathered before Him. He would pass judgment on them. Some would receive an inheritance prepared for them since the creation of the world and eternal life, but others would suffer the punishment of being separated from Him forever.

Jesus said He would decide what happens to every one of us at the end of time. Not only would He be the Judge, He would also be the criterion of judgment. What happens to us on the Day of Judgment depends on how we respond to Jesus in this life (Matthew 25:40, 45). Suppose the pastor at your local church were to get up in the pulpit and say, "On the Day of Judgment you will all appear before me; I will decide your eternal destiny. What happens to you will depend on how you've treated me and my followers." For a mere human being to make such a claim would be preposterous. Here we have another indirect claim to have the identity of Almighty God.

Direct claims

Christ. When the question was put to him, "Are you the Christ, the Son of the Blessed One?" Jesus said, "'I am ... and you will see the Son of Man sitting at the right hand of the Mighty One and coming on the clouds of heaven.' The high priest tore his clothes.'Why do we need any more witnesses?' he asked. 'You have heard the blasphemy. What do you think?'" (Mark 14:61-64). In this account, it appears Jesus was condemned to death for the assertion He made about Himself. A claim tantamount to a claim to be God was blasphemy in Jewish eyes, worthy of death.

God the Son. On one occasion, when the Jews started to stone Jesus, He asked, "Why are you stoning me?" They replied that they were stoning Him for blasphemy "'because you, a mere man, *claim to be God*'" (John 10:33, italics mine). His enemies clearly thought that this was exactly what He was declaring.

When Thomas, one of His disciples, knelt down before Jesus and said, "My Lord and my God" (John 20:28), Jesus didn't turn to him and say, "No, no, don't say that; I am not God." He said, "Because you have seen me, you have believed; blessed are those who have not seen and yet have believed" (John 20:29). He rebuked Thomas for being so slow to get the point.

Claims like these need to be tested. All sorts of people make all

31

kinds of claims. The mere fact that somebody claims to be someone does not mean that the claim is right. Many people, some in psychiatric hospitals, are deluded. They think they are Napoleon or the Pope, but they are not.

So how can we test people's claims? Jesus claimed to be the unique Son of God; God made flesh. There are three logical possibilities. If the claims were untrue, either He knew they were untrue, in which case He was an imposter, and an evil one at that. That is the first possibility. Or He did not know, in which case He was deluded; indeed, He was mad. That is the second possibility. The third possibility is that the claims were true.

C. S. Lewis put it like this:

> A man who was merely a man and said the sort of things Jesus said would not be a great moral teacher. He would either be a lunatic, on a level with the man who says he is a poached egg, or else he would be the Devil of Hell. You must make your choice. Either this man was, and is, the Son of God; or else a madman or something worse ... but let us not come up with any patronizing nonsense about His being a great human teacher. He has not left that open to us. He did not intend to.[13]

WHAT EVIDENCE IS THERE TO SUPPORT WHAT HE SAID?

In order to assess which of these three possibilities is right we need to examine the evidence that we have about His life.

His teaching

The teaching of Jesus is widely acknowledged to be the greatest teaching that has ever fallen from anyone's lips. Some who are not Christians say, "I love the Sermon on the Mount; I live by it." (If they read it they would realize that this is easier to say than to do, but they acknowledge that the Sermon on the Mount is great teaching.)

Bernard Ramm, an American professor of theology, said this about the teachings of Jesus:

> They are read more, quoted more, loved more, believed more, and translated more because they are the greatest words ever spoken ... Their greatness lies in the pure lucid spirituality in dealing clearly, definitively, and authoritatively with the greatest problems that throb in the human breast ... No other man's words have the appeal of Jesus' words because no other man can answer these fundamental human questions as Jesus answered them. They are the kind of words and the kind of answers we would expect God to give.[14]

Jesus' teaching is the foundation of our entire civilization in the West. Many of the laws in England and North America were originally based on the teachings of Jesus. We are making progress in virtually every field of science and technology. We travel faster and know more, and yet in nearly two thousand years no one has improved on the moral teaching of Jesus Christ. Could that teaching really have come from a con man or a madman?

His works

Jesus said that the miracles He performed were in themselves evidence that "the Father is in me, and I in the Father" (John 10:38).

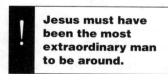

Jesus must have been the most extraordinary man to be around.

Jesus must have been the most extraordinary man to be around. Sometimes people say that Christianity is boring. Well, it was not boring being with Jesus.

When He went to a party, He turned water into wine (John 2:1-11). He received one person's picnic and multiplied it so that it could feed thousands (Mark 6:30-44). He had control over the elements and could speak to the wind and the waves and thereby stop a storm (Mark 4:35-41). He carried out the most remarkable healings: opening blind eyes, causing the deaf and dumb to hear and speak, and enabling the paralyzed to walk again. When He visited a hospital, a man who had been an invalid for thirty-eight years was able to pick up his bed and walk (John 5:1-9). He set people free from evil forces that had dominated their lives. On occasion, He even brought those who had died back to life (John 11:38-44).

Yet it was not just His miracles that made His work so impressive. It was His love, especially for the loveless (for instance, the lepers and the prostitutes), that seemed to motivate all that He did. Supremely it was His love shown on the cross (which, as we shall see in the next chapter, was the chief reason for His coming to earth). When they tortured Him and nailed Him to the cross, He said, "Father, forgive them, for they do not know what they are doing" (Luke 23:34). Surely these are not the activities of an evil or deluded man?

His character

The character of Jesus has impressed millions who would not call themselves Christians. For example, Bernard Levin wrote of Jesus:

> Is not the nature of Christ, in the words of the New Testament, enough to pierce to the soul anyone with a soul to be pierced? ... he still looms over the world, his message still clear, his pity still infinite, his consolation still effective, his words still full of glory, wisdom and love.[15]

One of my favorite descriptions of the character of Jesus comes from the former Lord Chancellor, Lord Hailsham. In his autobiographical *The Door Wherein I Went*, he describes how the person of Jesus came alive to him when he was in college:

> The first thing we must learn about him is that we should have

34

been absolutely entranced by his company. Jesus was irresistibly attractive as a man … What they crucified was a young man, vital, full of life and the joy of it, the Lord of life itself, and even more the Lord of laughter, someone so utterly attractive that people followed him for the sheer fun of it … the Twentieth Century needs to recapture the vision of this glorious and happy man whose mere presence filled his companions with delight. No pale Galilean he, but a veritable Pied Piper of Hamelin who would have the children laughing all round him and squealing with pleasure and joy as he picked them up.[16]

Here was a man who exemplified supreme unselfishness but never self-pity; humility but not weakness; joy but never at another's expense; kindness but not indulgence. He was a man in whom even His enemies could find no fault and where friends who knew Him well said He was without sin. Surely no one could suggest that a man with a character like that was evil or unbalanced?

His fulfillment of Old Testament prophecy

Wilbur Smith, the American writer on theological topics, said:

The ancient world had many different devices for determining the future, known as divination, but not in the entire gamut of Greek and Latin literature, even though they used the words prophet and prophecy, can we find any real specific prophecy of a great historic event to come in the distant future, nor any prophecy of a Saviour to arrive in the human race … Mohammedanism cannot point to any prophecies of the coming of Mohammed uttered hundreds of years before his birth. Neither can the founders of any cult in this country rightly identify any ancient text specifically foretelling their appearance.[17]

Yet in the case of Jesus, He fulfilled over three hundred prophecies (spoken by different voices over five hundred years), including

35

twenty-nine major prophecies fulfilled in a single day—the day He died. Although some of these prophecies may have found fulfillment at one level in the prophet's own day, they found their ultimate fulfillment in Jesus Christ.

I suppose it could be suggested that Jesus was a clever con man who deliberately set out to fulfill these prophecies in order to show that He was the Messiah foretold in the Old Testament.

The problem with that suggestion is, first, the sheer number of them would have made it extremely difficult. Secondly, humanly speaking He had no control over many of the events. For example, the exact manner of His death was foretold in the Old Testament (Isaiah 53), and also the place of His burial and even the place of His birth (Micah 5:2). Suppose Jesus had been a con man wanting to fulfill all these prophecies. It would have been a bit late by the time He discovered the place in which He was supposed to have been born!

His Resurrection

The physical resurrection from the dead of Jesus Christ is the cornerstone of Christianity. But what is the evidence that it really happened? I want to summarize the evidence under four main headings.

1. His absence from the tomb. Many theories have been put forward to explain the fact that Jesus' body was absent from the tomb on the first Easter Day, but none of them is very convincing.

First, it has been suggested that Jesus did not die on the cross. There was once a headline in *Today* newspaper: "Jesus did not die on the cross." Dr. Trevor Lloyd Davies claimed that Jesus was still alive when He was taken from the cross and that He later recovered.

Jesus had undergone a Roman flogging, under which many had died. He had been nailed to a cross for six hours. Could a man in this condition push away a stone weighing probably a ton and a half? The soldiers were clearly convinced that He was dead or they would not have taken His body down. If they had allowed a prisoner to escape, they would have been liable to the death penalty.

Furthermore, when the soldiers discovered that Jesus was already dead, "one of the soldiers pierced Jesus' side with a spear, bringing a sudden flow of blood and water" (John 19:34). This appears to be the separation of clot and serum, which we know today is strong medical evidence that Jesus was dead. John did not write it for that reason; he would not have possessed that knowledge, which makes it even more powerful evidence that Jesus was indeed dead.

Secondly, it has been argued that the disciples stole the body. Some have suggested that the disciples stole the body and began a rumor that Jesus had risen from the dead. Leaving aside the fact that the tomb was guarded, this theory is psychologically improbable. The disciples were depressed and disillusioned at the time of Jesus' death. It would have needed something extraordinary to transform the apostle Peter into the man who preached at Pentecost when three thousand people were converted.

In addition, when one considered how much they had to suffer for what they believed (floggings, torture, and for some even death), it seems inconceivable that they would be prepared to endure all that for something they knew to be untrue. I have a friend who was a scientist at Cambridge University who became a Christian because, as he examined the evidence, he was convinced that the disciples would not have been willing to die for what they knew to be a lie.

If the authorities had stolen the body, why did they not produce it?

Thirdly, some have said that the authorities stole the body. This seems the least probable theory of all. If the authorities had stolen the body, why did they not produce it when they were trying to quash the rumor that Jesus had risen from the dead?

Perhaps the most fascinating piece of evidence relating to Jesus' absence from the tomb is John's description of the grave clothes. In a way, the "empty tomb" is a misnomer. When Peter and John went to the tomb, they saw the grave clothes which were, as the Christian apologist Josh McDowell put it in *The Resurrection Factor*, "like the empty chrysalis of a caterpillar's cocoon" when the butterfly has emerged.[18] It was as if Jesus had simply passed through the grave clothes. Not surprisingly, John saw and believed (John 20:8).

2. His appearances to the disciples. Were these hallucinations? The Concise Oxford Dictionary describes an hallucination as an "apparent perception of external object not actually present." Hallucinations normally occur in highly strung, highly imaginative, and very nervous people, or in people who are sick or on drugs. The disciples do not fit into any of these categories. Burly fishermen, tax collector, and skeptics like Thomas are unlikely to hallucinate. People who hallucinate would be unlikely suddenly to stop doing so. Jesus appeared to His disciples on eleven different occasions over a period of six weeks. The number of occasions and the sudden cessation make the hallucination theory highly improbable.

Furthermore, over 500 people saw the risen Jesus. It is possible for one person to hallucinate. Maybe it is possible for two or three people to share the same hallucination. But is it likely that 500 people would all share the same hallucination?

Finally, hallucinations are subjective. There is no objective reality; it is like seeing a ghost. Jesus could be touched, He ate a piece of broiled fish (Luke 24:42, 43,) and on one occasion He cooked breakfast for the disciples (John 21:1-14). Peter says, "[They] ate and drank with him after he rose from the dead" (Acts 10:41). He held long conversations with them, teaching them many things about the kingdom of God (Acts 1:3).

3. The immediate effect. The effect of Jesus rising from the dead, as one would expect, had a dramatic impact on the world. The church was born and grew at a tremendous rate. As Michael Green, writer of many popular and scholarly works, puts it:

> [The] Church ... beginning from a handful of uneducated fishermen and tax gatherers, swept across the whole known world in the next three hundred years. It is a perfectly amazing story of peaceful revolution that has no parallel in the history of the world. It came about because Christians were able to say to inquirers: "Jesus did not only die for you. He is alive! You can meet him and discover for yourself the reality we are talking about!" They did, and joined the church and the church, born from that Easter grave, spread everywhere.[19]

4. Christian experience. Countless millions of people down through the ages have experienced the risen Jesus Christ. They consist of people of every color, race, tribe, continent, and nationality. They come from different economic, social, and intellectual backgrounds. Yet they all unite in a common experience of the risen Jesus Christ. Wilson Carlile, who was head of the Church Army in England, was preaching at Hyde Park Corner. He was saying, "Jesus Christ is alive today." One of the hecklers shouted out to him, "How do you know?"

Wilson Carlile replied, "Because I was speaking to Him for half an hour this morning!"

Millions of Christians all over the world today are experiencing a relationship with the risen Jesus Christ. During more than twenty years I, too, have found in my experience that Jesus Christ is alive today. I have experienced His love, His power, and a reality of a relationship that convinces me that He is really alive.

The evidence that Jesus rose from the dead is very extensive. A former Chief Justice of England, Lord Darling, said, "In its favour as living truth there exists such overwhelming evidence, positive and negative, factual and circumstantial, that no intelligent jury in the world could fail to bring in a verdict that the resurrection story is true."[20]

We saw when we looked earlier in the chapter at what Jesus said about himself, that there were only three realistic possibilities— either He was and is the Son of God, or else He was a madman or something worse. When one looks at the evidence it does not make sense to say that He was mad or evil. The whole weight of His teaching, His works, His character, His fulfillment of Old Testament prophecy, and His conquest of death make those suggestions absurd, illogical and unbelievable. On the other hand, they lend the strongest possible support to Jesus' own consciousness of being a man whose identity was God.

Either He was and is the Son of God or else He was a madman or ... worse.

C. S. Lewis sums it up like this:

We are faced then with a frightening alternative. The man we are talking about was (and is) just what he said or else a lunatic or something worse. Now it seems to me obvious that he was neither a lunatic nor a fiend; and consequently, however strange or terrifying or unlikely it may seem, I have to accept the view that he was

40

and is God. God has landed on this enemy occupied world in human form.[21]

3 Why Did Jesus Die?

Many people today go around with a cross on their earrings, bracelet, or necklace. We are so used to seeing this that we are not shocked by it. We might be shocked if we saw someone wearing a gallows or an electric chair on a chain; but the cross was just as much a form of execution. Indeed, it was one of the cruelest forms of execution known to mankind. It was abolished in 315 A.D. because even the Romans considered it too inhumane.

Yet the cross has always been regarded as the symbol of the Christian faith. A high proportion of the Gospels is about the death of Jesus. Much of the rest of the New Testament is concerned with explaining what happened on the cross. The central service of the church, the communion service, centers on the broken body and shed blood of Jesus. Churches are often built in the shape of a cross. When the apostle Paul went to Corinth he said, "I resolved to know nothing while I was with you except Jesus Christ and him crucified" (1 Corinthians 2:2). Most leaders who have influenced nations or impacted the world are remembered for the impact of their lives; Jesus, who more than any other person changed the face of world history, is remembered not so much for His life but for His death.

Why is there such concentration on the death of Jesus? What is the difference between His death and the death of Socrates, or one of the martyrs, or war heroes? Why did He die? What did it achieve? What does it mean when the New Testament says He died for our sins? These are some of the questions I want to try to answer in this chapter.

THE PROBLEM

Sometimes people say, "I have no need for Christianity." They say something along the lines of, "I am quite happy, my life is full and I try to be nice to other people and lead a good life." In order to understand why Jesus died we have to go back and look at the greatest problem that confronts every person.

If we are honest, we would all have to admit that we do things that we know are wrong. Paul wrote, "All have sinned and fall short of the glory of God" (Romans 3:23). In other words, relative to God's standards we all fall a long way short. If we compare ourselves to armed robbers or child molesters or even our neighbors, we may think we look good. But when we compare ourselves to Jesus Christ, we see how far short we fall. Somerset Maugham once said, "If I wrote down every thought I have ever thought and every deed I have ever done, men would call me a monster of depravity."

If we are honest, we all have to admit we do things that we know are wrong.

The essence of sin is rebellion against God (Genesis 3) and its result is that we are cut off from Him. Like the prodigal son (Luke 15), we find ourselves far from our Father's home and with our lives in a mess. Sometimes people say, "If we are all in the same boat, does it really matter?" The answer is that it does matter because of the consequences of sin in our lives, which can be summarized under four headings.

The pollution of sin

Jesus said, "What comes out of a man is what makes him 'unclean.' For from within, out of men's hearts, come evil thoughts, sexual immorality, theft, murder, adultery, greed, malice, deceit, lewdness, envy, slander, arrogance and folly. All these evils come from inside and make a man "'unclean'" (Mark 7:20-23). These things pollute our lives.

You may say, "I do not do most of these things." But one of them alone is enough to mess up our lives. We might wish the Ten Commandments were like an examination paper in which we only have to "attempt any three" of them. The New Testament says that if we break *any* part of the Law we are guilty of breaking *all* of it (James 2:10). It is not possible, for example, to have a "reasonably clean" driving record. Either it is clean or it is not. One driving offense stops it from being a clean record. So it is with us. One offense makes our lives unclean.

The power of sin

The things we do wrong have an addictive power. Jesus said, "Everyone who sins is a slave to sin" (John 8:34). It is easier to see this in

some areas of our wrongdoing than in others. For example, it is well known that if someone has taken a hard drug like heroin, it soon becomes an addiction.

It is also possible to be addicted to bad temper, envy, arrogance, pride, selfishness, slander, or sexual immorality. We can become addicted to patterns of thought or behavior which, on our own, we cannot break. This is the slavery that Jesus spoke about, and which has a destructive power in our lives.

Bishop J. C. Ryle, a former bishop of Liverpool, once wrote:

> Each and all [sins] have crowds of unhappy prisoners bound hand and foot in their chains … The wretched prisoners … boast sometimes that they are eminently free … There is no slavery like this. Sin is indeed the hardest of all task-masters. Misery and disappointment by the way, despair and hell in the end—these are the only wages that sin pays to its servants.[22]

The penalty for sin

Something within human nature cries out for justice. When we hear of children being molested, old people attacked in their homes, babies battered and the like, we long for the people who have done these things to be caught and punished. Our motives may be mixed: there may be an element of revenge. But there is such a thing as justifiable anger. We are right to feel that sins should be punished; that people who do such things should not get away with them.

It is not just other people's sins that deserve punishment. It is our own as well. One day we will all be subject to the judgment of God. Paul tells us that "the wages of sin is death" (Romans 6:23).

The partition of sin

The death Paul speaks of is not only physical. It is a spiritual death that results in eternal isolation from God. This cutting off from God begins now. The prophet Isaiah proclaimed, "Surely the arm of the Lord is not too short to save, nor his ear too dull to hear. But your iniquities have separated you from your God; your sins have hidden his face from you, so that he will not hear" (Isaiah 59:1, 2). The things we do wrong cause this barrier.

THE SOLUTION

We all have a need to deal with the problem of sin in our lives. The greater our understanding of our need the more we will appreciate what God has done.

The "self-substitution" of God

The Lord Chancellor, Lord Mackay of Clashfern, wrote: "The central theme of our faith is the sacrifice of himself by our Lord Jesus Christ on the cross for our sins.... The deeper our appreciation of our own need the greater will be our love for the Lord Jesus and, therefore, the more fervent our desire to serve him."[23] The good news of Christianity is that God loves us and He did not leave us in the mess that we make of our own lives. He came to earth, in the person of His Son Jesus to die instead of us (2 Corinthians 5:21; Galatians 3:13). This is what John Stott, author of many books and Rector Emeritus of All Souls Church, Langham Place in England, calls the "self-substitution of God." In the words of the apostle Peter, "*He* himself bore *our* sins in *his* body on the tree ... by *his* wounds you have been healed" (1 Peter 2:24, italics mine).

What does self-substitution mean? In his book *Miracle on the River Kwai*, Ernest Gordon tells the true story of a group of POWs working on the Burma Railway during World War II. At the end of each day the tools were collected from the work party. On one occasion, a Japanese guard shouted that a shovel was missing and demanded to know which man had taken it. He began to rant and rave, working himself up into a paranoid fury and ordered whoever was guilty to step forward. No one moved. "All die! All die!" he shrieked, cocking and aiming his rifle at the prisoners. At that moment one man stepped forward and the guard clubbed him to death with a rifle while he stood silently at attention. When they returned to the camp, the tools were counted again and no shovel was missing. That one man had gone forward as a substitute to save the others.

The agony of the Cross

In the same way Jesus came as our substitute. He endured crucifixion for us. Cicero described crucifixion as "the most cruel and hideous of tortures." Jesus was stripped and tied to a whipping post. He was flogged with four or five thongs of leather interwoven with sharp jagged bone and lead. Eusebius, the third-century church historian, described Roman flogging in these terms: the sufferer's "veins were laid bare, and ... the very muscles, sinews and bowels of the victim were open to exposure." Jesus was then taken to the Praetorium where a crown of thorns was thrust onto His head. He was mocked by a battalion of six hundred men and hit about the face and head. He was then forced to carry a heavy cross bar on His bleeding shoulders until He collapsed, and Simon of Cyrene was forced into carrying it for Him.

When they reached the site of crucifixion, He was again stripped naked. He was laid on the cross, and six-inch nails were driven into His forearms, just above the wrist. His knees were twisted sideways so that the ankles could be nailed between the tibia and the Achilles' tendon. He was lifted up on the cross,

The worst part of His suffering was not the physical or emotional pain ...

which was then dropped into a socket in the ground. There He was left to hang in intense heat and unbearable thirst, exposed to the ridicule of the crowd. He hung in unthinkable pain for six hours while His life slowly drained away.

Yet the worst part of His suffering was not the physical trauma or torture of crucifixion nor even the emotional pain of being rejected by the world and deserted by His friends, but the spiritual agony of being cut off from His Father for us as He carried our sins.

THE RESULT

Like a beautiful diamond the cross has many facets. On the cross, the powers of evil were disarmed (Colossians 2:15). Death and demonic powers were defeated. On the cross, God revealed His love for us. He showed that He is not a God who is aloof from suffering. He is "the crucified God" (as the title of the book by the German theologian Jurgen Moltmann puts it). He has entered our world and knows and understands all about suffering. On the cross, Jesus sets us an example of self-sacrificial love (1 Peter 2:21). Each of these aspects deserves a chapter of its own, which space does not allow. I want to concentrate on four images that the New Testament uses to describe what Jesus did on the cross for us. As John Stott points out, each of them is taken from a different area of day-to-day life.

The law court

The first image comes from *the law court*. Paul says that through Christ's death "we have been justified" (Romans 5:1). Justification is a legal term. If you went to court and were legally acquitted, you would be justified.

Two people went through school and college together and developed a close friendship. Life went on and they went their different ways and lost contact. One went on to become a judge, while the other one went down and down and ended up a criminal. One day the criminal appeared before the judge. He had committed a crime to which he pleaded guilty. The judge recognized his old friend and faced a dilemma. He was a judge, so he had to be just; he couldn't let the man off. On the other hand, he didn't want to punish the man, because he loved him. So he told his friend that he would fine him the correct penalty for the offense. That is justice. Then he came down from his position as judge and he wrote a check for the amount of the fine. He gave it to his friend, saying that he would pay the penalty for him. That is love.

This is an illustration of what God has done for us. In His justice, He judges us because we are guilty, but then, in His love, He came down in the person of His Son Jesus Christ and paid the penalty for us. In this way He is both "just"(in that He does not allow the guilty to go unpunished) and "the one who justifies" (Romans 3:26, in that by taking the penalty Himself, in the person of His Son, He enables us to go free). He is both our Judge and our Savior. It is not an innocent third party but God Himself who saves us. In effect, He gives us a check and says we have a choice: do we want Him to pay it for us, or are we going to face the judgment of God for our own wrongdoing?

The illustration I have used is not an exact one for three reasons. First, our plight is worse. The penalty we are facing is not just a fine, but death. Secondly, the relationship is closer. This is not just two friends: it is our Father in heaven who loves us more than any earthly father loves his own child. Thirdly, the cost was greater: it cost God not money, but His one and only Son, who paid *the penalty of sin*.

The marketplace

The second image comes from *the marketplace*. Debt is not a problem confined to the present day; it was a problem in the ancient world as well. If someone had serious debts, he might be forced to sell himself into slavery in order to pay them off. Suppose a man was standing in the marketplace, offering himself as a slave. Someone might have pity on him and ask, "How much do you owe?" The debtor might say, "ten thousand." Suppose the customer offers to pay the ten thousand and then lets him go free. In doing so, he would be "redeeming him" by paying a "ransom price."

In a similar way, for us "redemption ... came by Christ Jesus" (Romans 3:24). Jesus, by His death on the cross, paid the ransom price (Mark 10:45). In this way, we are set free from the power of sin. This is true freedom. Jesus said, "If the Son sets you free, you will be free indeed" (John 8:36). It is not that we never sin again, but that sin's hold over us is broken.

Billy Nolan was an alcoholic for thirty-five years. For twenty years he sat outside Holy Trinity Brompton Church drinking alcohol, begging for money. On May 13, 1990, he looked in the mirror and said, "You're not the Billy Nolan I once knew." To use his own expression, he asked the Lord Jesus Christ into his life and made a covenant with Him that he would never drink alcohol again. He has not touched a drop since. His life is transformed. He radiates the love and joy of Christ. I once said to him, "Billy, you look

> **!** It is not an innocent third party but God Himself who saves us.

happy." He replied, "I am happy because I am free. Life is like a maze and at last I have found a way out through Jesus Christ." Jesus' death on the cross made this freedom from the power of sin possible.

The temple

The third image comes from *the temple.*The Old Testament laid down very careful laws as to how sins should be dealt with. A whole system of sacrifices demonstrated the seriousness of sin and the need for being cleansed.

In a typical case the sinner would take an animal. The animal was to be as near perfection as possible. The sinner would lay his hands on the animal and confess his sins. Thus the sins were seen to pass from the sinner to the animal, which was then killed.

The writer of Hebrews points out that it is "impossible for the blood of bulls and goats to take away sins" (Hebrews 10:4). It was only a picture or a "shadow" (Hebrews 10:1). The reality came with the sacrifice of Jesus. Only the blood of Christ, our substitute, can take away our sin, because He alone was the perfect sacrifice, since He alone lived a perfect life. His blood "purifies us from all sin" (1 John 1:7) and removes *the pollution of sin.*

The home

The fourth image comes from *the home.* We saw that both the root and the result of sin was a broken relationship with God. The result of the Cross is the possibility of a restored relationship with God. Paul says that "*God was* reconciling the world to himself *in Christ*" (2 Corinthians 5:19, italics mine). Some people caricature the New Testament teaching and suggest that God is unjust because He punished Jesus, an innocent party, instead of us. This is not what the New Testament says. Rather, Paul says, "God was … in Christ." He was Himself the substitute in the person of His Son. He made it possible for us to be restored to a relationship with Him. *The partition of sin* has been destroyed. What happened to the prodigal son can happen to us. We can come back to the Father and experience His love and blessing. The relationship is not only for this life: it is eternal. One day we will be with the Father in heaven; we will be free, not only from the penalty for sin, the power of sin, the pollution of sin, and the partition of sin, but also from the presence of sin. God has made this possible through His self-substitution on the cross.

God loves each one of us so much and longs to be in a relationship with us as a human father longs to be in a relationship with each of his children. It is not just that Jesus died for everyone. He died for you and for me; it is very personal. Paul writes of "the Son of God, who loved me and gave himself for me" (Galatians 2:20). If you had been the only person in the world, Jesus would have died for you. Once we see the Cross in these personal terms, our lives will be transformed.

John Wimber, an American pastor and church leader, describes how the Cross became a personal reality to him:

After I had studied the Bible … for about three months I could have passed an elementary exam on the cross. I understood there is one God who could be known in three Persons. I understood Jesus is fully God and fully man and he died on the cross for the sins of the world. But I didn't understand that I was a sinner. I thought I was a good guy. I knew I messed up here and there but I didn't realize how serious my condition was.

But one evening around this time Carol [his wife] said, "I think it's time to do something about all that we've been learning." Then, as I looked on in utter amazement, she knelt down on the floor and started praying to what seemed to me to be the ceiling plaster. "Oh God," she said, "I am sorry for my sin."

I couldn't believe it. Carol was a better person than I, yet she thought she was a sinner. I could feel her pain and the depth of her prayers. Soon she was weeping and repeating, "I am sorry for my sin." There were six or seven people in the room, all with their eyes closed. I looked at them and then it hit me: They've all prayed this prayer too! I started sweating bullets. I thought I was going to die. The perspiration ran down my face and I thought, "I'm not going to do this. This is dumb. I'm a good guy." Then it struck me. Carol wasn't praying to the plaster; she was praying to a person, to a God who could hear her. In comparison to him she knew she was a sinner in need of forgiveness.

In a flash the cross made personal sense to me. Suddenly I knew something that I had never known before; I had hurt God's feelings. He loved me and in his love for me he sent Jesus. But I had turned away from that love; I had shunned it all of my life. I was a sinner, desperately in need of the cross.

Then I too was kneeling on the floor, sobbing, nose running, eyes watering, every square inch of my flesh perspiring profusely. I had this overwhelming sense that I was talking with someone who had been with me all of my life, but whom I failed to recognize. Like Carol, I began talking to the living God, telling him that I was a sinner but the only words I could say aloud were, "Oh God, Oh God."

I knew something revolutionary was going on inside of me. I thought, "I hope this works, because I'm making a complete fool of myself." Then the Lord brought to mind a man I had seen in Pershing Square in Los Angeles a number of years before. He was wearing a sign that said, "I'm a fool for Christ. Whose fool are you?" I thought at the time, "That's the most stupid thing I've ever seen." But as I kneeled on the floor I realized the truth of the odd sign: the cross is foolishness "to those who are perishing" (1 Corinthians 1:18). That night I knelt at the cross and believed in Jesus. I've been a fool for Christ ever since.[24]

If you are unsure about whether you have ever believed in Jesus, here is a prayer that you can pray as a way of starting the Christian life and receiving all the benefits that Christ died to make possible.

Heavenly Father, I am sorry for the things I have done wrong in my life. [Take a few moments to ask His forgiveness for anything particular that is on your conscience.] Please for-give me. I now turn from everything that I know is wrong.

Thank you that You sent Your Son, Jesus, to die on the cross for me so that I could be forgiven and set free. From now on I will follow and obey Him as my Lord.

Thank you that You now offer me this gift of forgiveness and Your Spirit. I now receive that gift.

Please come into my life by Your Holy Spirit to be with me forever. Through Jesus Christ, our Lord. Amen.

4 How Can I Be Sure of My Faith?

At the age of eighteen, in many ways my life could not have been better. I was halfway through my first year of college. I was having fun, and every opportunity of life seemed open to me. Christianity had no appeal for me; indeed the reverse. I felt that if I became a Christian, life would become very boring. I imagined God wanted to stop all the fun and make me do all sorts of tedious religious things.

On the other hand, as I looked at the evidence for Christianity, I became convinced it was true. I thought the answer was to delay the decision, enjoy life now, and become a Christian on my deathbed. Yet I knew I could not do that with integrity. Very reluctantly, I gave my life to Christ.

What I had failed to realize is that Christianity is about a relationship with God—a God who loves us and wants the very best for us. I was, to use the title of C. S. Lewis' book about his own experience of Christ, "surprised by joy." Becoming a Christian was the start of the most exciting relationship. Indeed, it was the start of a new life. As Paul wrote, "When someone becomes a Christian he becomes a brand new person inside. He is not the same any more. A new life has begun" (2 Corinthians 5:17, *The Living Bible*). I sometimes keep a note of what people say or write after they have just started the new life that Paul is speaking about. Here are two examples:

> I now have hope where previously there was only despair. I can forgive now, where before there was only coldness ... God is so alive for me. I can feel Him guiding me, and the complete and utter loneliness that I have been feeling is gone. God is filling a deep, deep void.

> I felt like hugging everybody in the street ... I cannot stop praying, I even missed my bus stop today because I was so busy praying on the top deck.

Experiences vary greatly. Some immediately know a difference. For others it is more gradual. What matters is not so much the experience as the fact that when we receive Christ, we become children of God. It is the start of a new relationship. As the apostle John writes, "Yet to all who received him, to those who believed in his name, he gave the right to become children of God" (John 1:12).

Good parents want their children to be sure about their relationship with them. In the same way, God wants us to be sure about our relationship with Him. Many people are uncertain about whether they are Christians or not. At the end of an *Alpha Course*, I asked people to fill out a questionnaire. One of the questions I asked was, "Would you have described yourself as a Christian at the beginning of the course?" Here is a list of some of the answers:

- "Yes, but without any real experience of a relationship with God."
- "Sort of."
- "Possibly yes/think so."
- "Not sure."
- "Probably."
- "Ish."
- "Yes, though looking back possibly no."
- "No, a semi-Christian."

The New Testament makes it clear that it is possible for us to be sure that we are Christians and that we have eternal life. The apostle John writes, "I write these things to you who believe in the name of the Son of God so that you may *know* that you have eternal life" (1 John 5:13, italics mine).

Just as three legs support a camera tripod, our assurance of our relationship with God stands firmly based on the activity of all three members of the Trinity: the promises that the Father gives us in His Word, the sacrifice of the Son for us on the cross, and the assurance of the Spirit in our hearts. These can be summarized under three headings: the Word of God, the work of Jesus, and the witness of the Holy Spirit.

THE WORD OF GOD

If we were to rely on our feelings, we could never be sure about anything. Our feelings go up and down depending on all sorts of factors, such as the weather or what we have had for breakfast. They are changeable and deceptive. The promises in the Bible, which is the Word of God, do not change and are totally reliable.

There are many great promises in the Bible. A verse that I found helpful, especially at the beginning of my Christian life, is one that comes in the last book of the Bible. In a vision the apostle John sees Jesus speaking to seven different churches. To the church in Laodicea Jesus says: "Here I am! I stand at the door and knock. If anyone hears my voice and opens the door, I will come in and eat with him, and he with me" (Revelation 3:20).

There are many ways of speaking about starting the new life of the Christian faith: "becoming a Christian," "giving our lives to Christ," "receiving Christ," "inviting Jesus into our lives," "believing in Him," and "opening the door to Jesus" are some of the variations. All of them describe the same reality: that Jesus enters our lives by the Holy Spirit, as is pictured in Revelation 3:20.

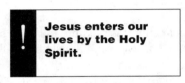

Jesus enters our lives by the Holy Spirit.

The Pre-Raphaelite artist Holman Hunt (1827–1910), inspired by this verse, painted "The Light of the World." He painted three versions in all. One hangs in Keble College, Oxford; another version is in the Manchester City Art Gallery; the most famous toured in 1905–1907 and was presented in June of 1908 to St. Paul's Cathedral, where it still hangs. When the first version was shown it received generally poor reviews. Then, on May 5, 1854, John Ruskin, the artist and critic, wrote to *The Times* and explained the symbolism at length and brilliantly defended it as "one of the very noblest works of sacred art ever produced in this or any other age."

Jesus, the Light of the World, stands at a door, which is overgrown with ivy and weeds. The door clearly represents the door of someone's life. This person has never invited Jesus to come into his or her life. Jesus is standing at the door and knocking. He is awaiting a response. He wants to come in and be part of that person's life. Apparently, someone said to Holman Hunt that he had made a mistake. They told him, "You have forgotten to paint a handle on the door." "Oh no," replied Hunt, "that is deliberate. There is only one handle and that is on the inside."

In other words, we have to open the door to let Jesus into our lives. Jesus will never force His way in. He gives us the freedom to choose. It is up to us whether or not we open the door to Him. If we do, He promises, "I will come in and eat with him and he with me." Eating together is a sign of the friendship that Jesus offers to all those who open the door of their lives to Him.

Once we have invited Jesus to come in, He promises that He will never leave us. He says to His disciples, "I am with you always" (Matthew 28:20). We may not always be in direct conversation with Him, but He will always be there. If you are working in a room with a friend, you may not be speaking to him directly, but you are nevertheless aware of his presence. This is how it is with the presence of Jesus. He is with us always.

This promise of the presence of Jesus with us is closely related to another marvelous promise that comes in the New Testament. Jesus promises to give His followers eternal life (John 10:28). As we have seen, eternal life in the New Testament is a quality of life that comes from living in a relationship with God through Jesus Christ (John 17:3). It starts in this life, when we experience the fullness of life that Jesus came to bring (John 10:10). Yet it is not just in this life; it goes on into eternity.

The resurrection of Jesus from the dead has many implications. First, it assures us about the past; that what Jesus achieved on the cross was effective. "The resurrection is not the reversal of a defeat, but the proclamation of a victory."[25] Secondly, it assures us about the present. Jesus is alive. His power is with us, bringing us life in all its fullness. Thirdly, it assures us about the future. This life is not the end; there is life beyond the grave. History is not meaningless or cyclical; it is moving towards a glorious climax.

One day Jesus will return to earth to establish a new heaven and a new earth (Revelation 21:1). Then those who are in Christ will go to "be with the Lord forever" (1 Thessalonians 4:17). There will be no more crying, for there will be no more pain. There will be no more temptation, for there will be no more sin. There will be no more suffering and no more separation from loved ones. Then we will see Jesus face to face (1 Corinthians 13:12). We will be given glorious and painless resurrection bodies (1 Corinthians 15). We will be transformed into the moral likeness of Jesus Christ (1 John 3:2). Heaven will be a place of intense joy and delight that goes on forever. Some have ridiculed this by suggesting it would be monotonous or boring. But: "No eye has seen, no ear has heard, no mind has conceived what God has prepared for those who love him" (1 Corinthians 2:9 quoting Isaiah 64:4).

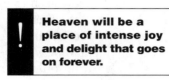

Heaven will be a place of intense joy and delight that goes on forever.

C. S. Lewis describes heaven in one of the stories from the *Chronicles of Narnia*:

> The term is over: the holidays have begun. The dream is ended: this is the morning ... all their life in this world ... had only been the cover and the title page: now at last they were beginning Chapter One of the Great Story which no one on earth has read: which goes on forever: in which every chapter is better than the one before.[26]

THE WORK OF JESUS

When I was in college, I came across a book called *Heaven, Here I Come*. At first I, like many today, thought this was an arrogant claim. It *would* be arrogant to be so confident if it depended on us. If my entry into heaven depended on how good a life I had led, I would not have any hope of getting in at all.

The wonderful news is that it does not depend on me. It depends on what Jesus has done for me. It depends not on what I do or achieve, but on His work on the cross. What He did on the cross enables Him to give us eternal life as a gift (John 10:28; Romans 6:23b). We do not earn a gift. We accept it with gratitude.

Although eternal life is free, it is not cheap. It cost Jesus His life. If we want to receive this gift, we have to be willing to turn our back on everything we know to be wrong. Theses are the things which do us harm and lead to "death" (Rom. 6:23a). Turning away from them is what the Bible calls *repentance* (literally changing our minds). We accept the gift through repentance and faith.

What is faith? John Patten (1824-1907), a Scot from Dumfriesshire, traveled to New Hebrides (a group of islands in the South-West Pacific) to tell the tribal people about Jesus. The islanders were cannibals and his life was in constant danger. Patten decided to work on a translation of John's gospel, but found that there was no word in their language for "belief" or "trust." Nobody trusted anybody else.

Eventually, Patten hit upon the way to find the word he was looking for. One day, when his native servant came in, Patten raised both feet off the floor, sat back in his chair, and asked, "What am I doing now?" In reply, the servant used a word which means, "to lean your whole weight upon." This was the expression Patten used. Faith is leaning our whole weight upon Jesus and what He has done for us on the cross.

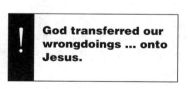

God transferred our wrongdoings ... onto Jesus.

It all starts with God's love for us: "For God so loved the world that he gave his one and only Son, that whoever believes in him shall not perish but have eternal life" (John 3:16). We all deserve to "perish." God, in His love for us, saw the mess we were in and gave His only Son, Jesus, to die for us. As a result of His death, everlasting life is offered to all who believe.

On the cross, Jesus took all our wrongdoing upon Himself. This had been prophesied in the Old Testament. In the Book of Isaiah, written hundreds of years beforehand, the prophet foresaw what "the suffering servant" would do for us and said: "We all, like sheep, have gone astray, each of us has turned to his own way; and the Lord has laid on him [that is, Jesus] the iniquity of us all" (Isaiah 53:6).

What the prophet is saying is that we have all done wrong; we have all gone astray. He says elsewhere that the things we do wrong cause a separation between us and God (Isaiah 59:1, 2). This is one of the reasons why God can seem remote. There is a barrier between us and Him that prevents us from experiencing His love.

On the other hand, Jesus never did anything wrong. He lived a perfect life. There was no barrier between Him and His Father. On the cross, God transferred our wrongdoings (our iniquity) onto Jesus ("the Lord has laid on him the iniquity of us all"). That is why Jesus cried out on the cross, "My God, my God, why have you forsaken me?" (Mark 15:34). At that moment He was cut off from God, not because of His own wrongdoing, but because of ours.

This made it possible for the barrier between us and God to be removed—for all who accept for themselves what Jesus has done for them. As a result, we can be sure of God's forgiveness. Our guilt has been taken. We can be sure that we will never be condemned. As Paul puts it, "Therefore, there is now no condemnation for those who are in Christ Jesus" (Romans 8:1). This, then, is the second reason we can be sure that we have eternal life: because of what Jesus achieved for us on the cross by dying for us.

THE WITNESS OF THE SPIRIT

When someone becomes a Christian, God's Holy Spirit comes to live within that person. There are two aspects in particular of the many activities of the Holy Spirit that help us to be sure of our faith in Christ.

First, He transforms us from within. He produces the character of Jesus in our lives. This is called "the fruit of the Spirit:" love, joy, peace, patience, kindness, goodness, faithfulness, gentleness, and self-control (Galatians 5:22, 23). When the Holy Spirit comes to live within us this fruit begins to grow.

Our character. Changes in our character should be observable by other people, but obviously these changes do not occur overnight. We have just planted a pear tree in our garden, and almost every day I look to see if it has any fruit. One day a friend of mine played a practical joke on me. He hung a large Granny Smith apple on the tree with cotton. Even I was not fooled by this. My limited knowledge of gardening tells me that fruit takes time to grow (and pear trees do not produce apples). We hope that over a period of time other people will notice that we are more loving, more joyful, more peaceful, more patient, more kind, and more self-controlled.

Our relationships. As well as changes in our character, there should be changes in our relationships, both with God and with other people. We develop a new love for God—Father, Son, and Holy Spirit. For example, hearing the word "Jesus" has a different emotional impact. Before I was a Christian, if I was listening to the radio or watching television and heard the subject change to Jesus Christ, I would probably have turned it off. After I became a Christian, I would turn the volume up, because my attitude toward Him had totally changed. This was a little sign of my new love for Him.

Our attitude toward others also changes. Often new Christians say to me that they are suddenly noticing the faces of people in the street and on the bus. Before they had little interest; now they feel a concern for people who often look sad and lost. I found that one of the biggest differences was in my attitude toward other Christians. I am afraid that beforehand I tended to avoid anyone who had a Christian faith. Afterwards, I found they were not as bad as I had expected! Indeed, I soon started to experience a depth of friendship with other Christians that I had never known in my life before.

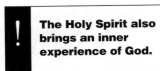

The Holy Spirit also brings an inner experience of God.

Secondly, as well as these changes that can be observed in our lives, the Holy Spirit also brings an inner experience of God. He creates a deep, personal conviction that we are children of God (Romans 8:15, 16). This experience is different for everyone.

66

Carl Tuttle is an American pastor who came from a broken home. He had a very unhappy childhood in which his father abused him. After he became a Christian, on one occasion he particularly wanted to hear what God was saying to him. He decided to go out into the country where he could pray for a whole day without being interrupted. So he arrived and began to pray. But after fifteen minutes he felt he was not getting anywhere. So he drove home again feeling very depressed and disappointed. He told his wife that he would go to see Zachary, his two-month-old baby. He went into the room and picked him up. As he was holding him he felt an incredible love welling up within him for this baby boy, and he started crying and talking to him. "Zachary," he said, "I love you. I love you with all my heart. No matter what happens in this life, I will never harm you, I'll always protect you. I'll always be your father, I'll always be your friend, I'll always care for you, I'll always nurture you, and I'll do this, no matter what sins you commit, no matter what you do, and no matter whether you turn from me or from God." Suddenly Carl sensed that he was in God's arms and that God was saying, "Carl, you are my son and I love you. No matter what you do, no matter where you go, I'll always care for you, I'll always provide for you, I'll always guide you."

In this way, the Spirit witnessed to Carl's spirit that he was a child of God (Romans 8:16). This is the third way in which we are assured of our relationship with God, and that we are forgiven and have eternal life. We know it because the Spirit of God witnesses to us, both objectively through an ongoing change in our character and relationships, and subjectively through a deep inner conviction that we are children of God.

In these ways (the Word of God, the work of Jesus, and the witness of the Spirit), those who believe in Jesus can be sure that they are children of God and that they have eternal life.

It is not arrogant to be sure. The certainty is based on what God has promised, on what Jesus died to achieve, and on the work of the

Holy Spirit in our lives. It is one of the privileges of being a child of God: to be able to be absolutely confident about our relationship with our Father; to be sure of the fact that we are forgiven; to be sure that we are Christians, and to know that we have eternal life.

5 Why and How Should I Read the Bible?

It was Valentine's Day night 1974. I had been to a party and was sitting in my room at college when my best friend came back with his girlfriend (now his wife). They told me that they had become Christians. I was immediately alarmed for them, thinking that the Moonies had lured them and they needed my help.

I was at times an atheist and at times an agnostic, unsure of what I believed. I had been baptized and confirmed, but neither experience had meant much to me. At school I had been to chapel regularly and studied the Bible in religious education lessons. But I had ended up rejecting it all and, indeed, arguing powerfully (or so I thought) against Christianity.

Now I wanted to help my friends, so I thought I would embark on a thorough research of the subject. I made a plan to read the Koran, Karl Marx, Jean-Paul Sartre (the existentialist philosopher), and the Bible. I happened to have a rather dusty copy of the Bible on my shelves, so that night I picked it up and started reading. I read all the way through Matthew, Mark, and Luke, and halfway through John's Gospel. Then I fell asleep. When I woke up, I finished John's Gospel and carried on through Acts, Romans, and 1 and 2 Corinthians. I was completely gripped by what I read. I had read it before and it had meant virtually nothing to me. This time it came alive and I could not put it down. It had a ring of truth about it. I knew as I read it that I had to respond, because it spoke so powerfully to me. Very shortly afterwards, I came to put my faith in Jesus Christ.

Since then the Bible has become a delight to me. According to the psalmist:

> Blessed is the man who does not walk in the counsel of the wicked or stand in the way of sinners or sit in the seat of mockers. But his delight is in the law of the Lord, and on his law he meditates day and night. He is like a tree planted by streams of water, which yields its fruit in season and whose leaf does not wither. Whatever he does prospers (Psalm 1:1-3).

I love that phrase, "His delight is in the law of the Lord." All the psalmist had at that stage was the first five books of the Bible. They were his delight. In this chapter I want to look at why and how the Bible can become a delight for each of us, looking, by way of introduction, at its uniqueness.

The Bible is uniquely popular

Bible sales amount to more than half a billion dollars a year in North America. The average American household has 3.2 Bibles. Twenty-seven percent of Americans own at least five Bibles. An article in *The Times* in London said, "Forget the modern British novelists and TV tie-ins; the Bible is the biggest-selling book every year." The writer remarked:

> As usual the top seller by several miles was the … Bible. If cumulative sales of the Bible were frankly reflected in bestseller lists, it would be a rare week when anything else would achieve a look in. It is wonderful, weird, or just plain baffling in this increasingly godless age—when the range of books available grows wider with each passing year—that this one book should go on selling hand over fist, month in, month out…. It is estimated that nearly 1,250,000 Bibles and Testaments are sold in the UK each year.

The writer ends by saying, "All versions of the Bible sell well all the time. Can the Bible Society offer an explanation? 'Well,' I am told disarmingly, 'it is such a good book.'"

The Bible is uniquely powerful

In May 1928, Prime Minister Stanley Baldwin said, "The Bible is a high explosive. But it works in strange ways and no living man can tell or know how that book, in its journey through the world, has startled the individual soul in ten thousand different places into a new life, a new world, a new belief, a new conception, a new faith."

In recent times there has been a rising interest in the occult. People play with ouija boards, see occult films, have their fortunes told, and read horoscopes. They want to get in touch with the supernatural. The tragedy is that they are seeking to communicate with supernatural evil forces, whereas what God offers us in the Bible is an opportunity to meet with the supernatural powers of good. To meet with the living God is so much more thrilling, more satisfying, and a great deal wiser.

The Bible is uniquely precious

About sixteen years ago I was on vacation with my family in central Asia, in part of the former USSR. At that time Bibles were strictly illegal there, but I took some Christian literature, including some Russian Bibles. While I was there, I went to churches and looked for people who seemed from their faces to be genuine Christians. (At that time the meetings were usually infiltrated by the KGB.) On one occasion I followed a man, who was probably in his sixties, down the street after a service. I went up to him and tapped him on the shoulder. There was nobody around. I took out one of my Bibles and handed it to him. For a moment he had an expression of almost disbelief. Then he took from his pocket a New Testament, which was probably a hundred years old. The pages were so threadbare they were virtually transparent. When he realized that he had received a whole Bible, he was elated. He didn't speak any English and I didn't speak any Russian. We hugged each other and he started to run down the street jumping for joy, because he knew that the Bible was the most precious thing in the world.

When he realized that he had received a whole Bible, he was elated.

Why is it so popular, so powerful, and so precious? Jesus said, "Man does not live on bread alone, but on every word that comes from the mouth of God" (Matthew 4:4). The verb is in the present tense, and means "is continually coming out of the mouth of God"; it is like a stream pouring forth and, like the stream of a fountain, is never static. God is continually wanting to communicate with His people. He does so primarily through the Bible.

A MANUAL FOR LIFE—GOD HAS SPOKEN

God has spoken to us through His Son, Jesus Christ (Hebrews 1:2). Christianity is a revealed faith. We cannot find out about God unless God reveals Himself. God has revealed Himself in a person, Jesus Christ. He is God's ultimate revelation.

The main way we know about Jesus is through God's revelation recorded in the Bible. Biblical theology should be the study of God's revelation in the Bible. God has also revealed Himself through creation (Romans 1:19, 20; Psalm 19). Science is an exploration of God's revelation in creation. (There should be no conflict between science and the Christian faith; rather they complement one another.) God also speaks to people directly by His Spirit: through prophecy, dreams, and visions, and through other people. We will look at all these in more detail later, especially in the chapter on guidance. In this chapter we will look at the way God speaks through the Bible.

Paul wrote of the inspiration of the Scriptures that were available to him: "All Scripture is God-breathed and is useful for teaching, rebuking, correcting and training in righteousness, so that the man of God may be thoroughly equipped for every good work" (2 Timothy 3:16, 17).

The word for "God-breathed" is *theopneustos*. It is often translated as "inspired by God"; but transliterated it is "God-breathed." The writer is saying that Scripture is God speaking. Of course He used human agents. The Bible is one hundred percent the work of human beings. But it is also one hundred percent inspired by God (just as Jesus is fully human and fully God).

The Bible is 100% the work of human beings and 100% inspired by God.

This is the way in which Jesus Himself treated the Scriptures of His day. For Him, what the Scriptures said, God said (Mark 7:5-13). If

Jesus is our Lord, our attitude toward the Scriptures should be the same as His. John Wenham, author of *Christ and the Bible*, says, "Belief in Christ as the supreme revelation of God leads to belief in scriptural inspiration—of the Old Testament by the direct testimony of Jesus and of the New Testament by inference from his testimony."[27]

This high view of the inspiration of the Bible has been held almost universally by the worldwide church down the ages. The early theologians of the church had this view. Irenaeus (about 130–200 A.D.) said, "The Scriptures are perfect." Likewise, the reformers, for example Martin Luther, spoke of "Scripture which has never erred." Today, the Roman Catholic official view is enshrined in Vatican II. The Scriptures "written under the inspiration of the Holy Spirit … have God as their author. …" Therefore they must be acknowledged as being without error. This also, until the last century, was the view of all Protestant churches throughout the world, and although today it is questioned and even ridiculed at a school level, it continues to be held by many fine scholars.

This does not mean that there are no difficulties in the Bible. Even Peter found some of Paul's letters "hard to understand" (2 Peter 3:16). There are moral and historical difficulties and some apparent contradictions.

The Bible was written over 1500 years by at least 40 different authors.

Some of the difficulties can be explained by the different contexts in which the authors were writing. It is important to remember that the Bible was written over a period of fifteen hundred years by at least forty authors, including kings, scholars, philosophers, fishermen, poets, statesmen, historians, and doctors. They wrote different types of literature, such as history, poetry, prophecy, apocalyptic, and letters.

Although some of the apparent contradictions can be explained by differing contexts, others are harder to resolve. This does not mean, however, that it is impossible and that we should abandon our belief in the inspiration of Scripture. Every great doctrine of the Christian faith has its difficulties. For example, it is hard to reconcile the love of God and the suffering in the world. Yet every Christian believes in the love of God and seeks an understanding of the problem of suffering within that framework. In a similar way we need to hold on to the belief in the inspiration of the Bible and try to understand the difficult passages within that context. It is important not to run away from the difficulties but to seek, so far as we can, to resolve them to our own satisfaction.

It is very important to hold on to the fact that *all* Scripture is inspired by God, even if we cannot immediately resolve all the difficulties. If we do, it should transform the way in which we live our lives. When Billy Graham was a young man several people started to say to him, "You can't believe everything in the Bible." He began to worry about it and started to become very muddled. John Pollock, in his biography of the evangelist, records what happened:

So I [Billy Graham] went back and I got my Bible, and I went out in the moonlight. And I got to a stump and put the Bible on the stump, and I knelt down, and I said, "Oh, God; I cannot prove certain things. I cannot answer some of the questions Chuck is raising and some of the other people are raising, but I accept this Book by faith as the Word of God." I stayed by the stump praying wordlessly, my eyes moist … I had a tremendous sense of God's presence. I had a great peace that the decision I had made was right.[28]

If we accept that the Bible is inspired by God, then its authority must follow from that. If it is God's Word, then it must be our supreme authority for what we believe and how we act. For Jesus, it was His supreme authority—above what the church leaders of His time said (see Mark 7:1-20) and above the opinions of others, however clever they were (see Mark 12:18-27). Having said that, we must of course give due weight to what church leaders and others say, provided it does not conflict with the revealed Word of God.

The Bible should be our authority in all matters of "creed and conduct." As we have seen, "All Scripture is God-breathed and is useful for teaching, rebuking, correcting and training in righteousness"

If the Bible is God's Word, then it must be our supreme authority …

(2 Timothy 3:16). First, it is our authority for what we believe (our creed), for "teaching" and "rebuking." It is in the Bible that we find what God says (and what we should, therefore, believe) about suffering, about Jesus, about the Cross, and so on.

Secondly, it is our authority for how we act (our conduct), for "correcting" and for "training in righteousness." It is here that we find out what is wrong in God's eyes and how we can live a righteous life. For instance, "The ten commandments … are a brilliant analysis of the minimum conditions on which a society, a people, a nation can live a sober, righteous and civilised life."29

Some things are very clear in the Bible. It tells us how to conduct our day-to-day lives, for example, when we're at work or under pressure. We know from the Bible that the single state can be a high calling (1 Corinthians 7:7, 8), but it is the exception rather than the rule; marriage is the norm (Genesis 2:24; 1 Corinthians 7:2). We know that sexual intercourse outside marriage is wrong. We know that it is right to try to get a job if we can. We know it is right to give and to forgive. We are also given, among other things, guidelines on how to bring up our children and to care for elderly relatives.

Some people say, "I don't want this rule book. It is too restrictive—all those regulations. I want to be free. If you live by the Bible, you are not free to enjoy life." But is that really right? Does the Bible take away our freedom? Or does it in fact give us freedom? Rules and regulations can in fact create freedom and increase enjoyment.

A few years ago, a soccer match had been arranged involving twenty-two small boys, including one of my sons, age eight at the time. A friend of mine called Andy (who had been training the boys all year) was going to referee. Unfortunately, by 2:30 P.M. he had not turned up. The boys could wait no longer. I was pressured into being the substitute referee. There were a number of difficulties with this: I had no whistle; there were no markings for the boundaries; I didn't know any of the other boys' names; they did not have uniforms to distinguish which sides they were on; and I did not know the rules nearly as well as some of the boys.

The game soon descended into complete chaos. Some shouted that the ball was in. Others said that it was out. I wasn't at all sure, so I let things run. Then the fouls started. Some cried, "Foul!" Others said, "No foul!" I didn't know who was right. So I let them play on. Then people began to get hurt. By the time Andy arrived, there were three boys lying injured on the ground and all the rest were shouting, mainly at me! But the moment Andy arrived, he blew his whistle, arranged the teams, told them where the boundaries were and had them under control. Then the boys had the game of their lives.

Were the boys more free without the rules or were they in fact less free? Without any effective authority they were free to do exactly what they wanted. The result was that people were confused and hurt. They much preferred it when they knew where the boundaries were. Within those boundaries they were free to enjoy the game.

In some ways the Bible is like that. It is God's rule book. He tells us what is "in" and what is "out." He tells us what we can do and what we must not do. If we play within the rules there is freedom and joy. When we break the rules, people get hurt. God did not say, "Do not murder" in order to ruin our enjoyment of life. He did not say, "Do not commit adultery" because He is a spoilsport. He did not want people to get hurt. When people leave their wives or husbands and children to commit adultery, lives get messed up.

The Bible is God's revelation of His will for His people. The more we discover His will and put it into practice, the freer we shall be. God has spoken. We need to hear what He has said.

A LOVE LETTER FROM GOD—GOD SPEAKS

For some people the Bible is never more than a well-thumbed manual for life. They believe God has spoken and they may study the Bible for hours. They analyze it, read commentaries on it (and there is nothing wrong with that), but they do not seem to realize that not only has God spoken, but He still speaks today through what He has said in the Bible. God's desire is that we should live in a relationship with Him. He wants to speak to us daily through His Word. So as well as being a manual for life, the Bible is a love letter.

The main point of the Bible is to show us how to enter into a relationship with God through Jesus Christ. Jesus said, "You diligently study the Scriptures because you think that by them you possess

78

eternal life. These are the Scriptures that testify about me, yet you refuse to come to me to have life" (John 5:39, 40).

Dr. Christopher Chavasse, formerly Bishop of Rochester, said:

> The Bible is the portrait of our Lord Jesus Christ. The Gospels are the figure itself in the portrait. The Old Testament is the background leading up to the divine figure, pointing towards it and absolutely necessary to the composition as a whole. The Epistles serve as the dress and accoutrements of the figure, explaining and describing it. Then, while by our Bible reading we study the portrait as a great whole, the miracle happens, the figure comes to life and stepping down from the canvas of the written word, the everlasting Christ of the Emmaus story becomes himself our Bible teacher, to interpret to us in all the Scriptures the things concerning himself.

It is no good studying the Bible if we never come to Jesus Christ; if we never meet with Him as we read it. Martin Luther said, "Scripture is the manger or 'cradle' in which the infant Jesus lies. Don't let us inspect the cradle and forget to worship the baby."

Our relationship with God is two-way. We speak to Him in prayer and He speaks to us in many ways, but especially through the Bible. God speaks through what He has spoken. When he quotes the Old Testament, the writer of Hebrews says, "As the Holy Spirit *says*" (Hebrews 3:7). It is not just that the Holy Spirit spoke in the past. He speaks afresh through what He spoke. This is what makes the Bible so alive. Again, as Martin Luther put it, "The Bible is alive, it speaks to me; it has feet, it runs after me; it has hands, it lays hold on me."

What happens when God speaks? *First, He brings faith to those who are not yet Christians.* Paul says, "Faith comes from hearing the message, and the message is heard through the word of Christ" (Romans 10:17). It is often as people read the Bible that they come to faith in Jesus Christ. That was certainly my experience.

David Suchet, a leading British Shakespearean actor and well known for his role as Agatha Christie's Hercule Poirot, tells how he was lying in his bathtub in a hotel in the United States when he had a sudden and impulsive desire to read the Bible. He managed to find a Gideon Bible and he started to read the New Testament. As he read, he came to put his faith in Jesus Christ. He said:

> From somewhere I got this desire to read the Bible again. That's the most important part of my conversion. I started with the Acts of the Apostles and then moved to Paul's Letters—Romans and Corinthians. And it was only after that I came to the gospels. In the New Testament I suddenly discovered the way that life should be followed.[30]

Secondly, he speaks to Christians. As we read the Bible we experience a transforming relationship with God through Jesus Christ. Paul says, "We, who with unveiled faces all reflect the Lord's glory, are being transformed into his likeness with ever-increasing glory, which comes from the Lord, who is the Spirit" (2 Corinthians 3:18).

As we study the Bible, we come into contact with Jesus Christ. It has always struck me as the most extraordinarily wonderful fact that we can speak to and hear from the person whom we read about in the pages of the New Testament—the same Jesus Christ. He will speak to us (not audibly, on the whole, but in our hearts) as we read the Bible. We will hear His message for us. As we spend time with Him, our characters will become more like His.

Spending time in His presence, listening to His voice, brings many blessings. He often brings joy and peace, even in the middle of a crisis in our lives (Psalm 23:5). When we are not sure which direction we should go in, God often guides us through His Word (Psalm 119:105). The Book of Proverbs even tells us that God's words bring healing to our bodies (Proverbs 4:22).

The Bible also provides us with a defense against spiritual attack. We only have one detailed example of Jesus facing temptation. Jesus faced intense attack by the devil at the start of His ministry (Matthew 4:1-11). Jesus met every temptation with a verse from the Scriptures. I find it fascinating that every one of His replies came from Deuteronomy 6–8. It seems plausible to infer that Jesus had been studying this portion of Scripture and that it was fresh in His mind.

The Word of God has great power. The writer of the Book of Hebrews says, "The word of God is living and active. Sharper than any double-edged sword, it penetrates even to dividing soul and spirit, joints and marrow; it judges the thoughts and attitudes of the heart" (Hebrews 4:12). It has power to pierce all our defenses and get through to our hearts. I remember once reading Philippians 2:4,

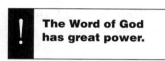

The Word of God has great power.

"Each of you should look not only to your own interests, but also to the interests of others." It was like an arrow going straight into me as I realized how selfish I was being. In these and many other ways, God's Word speaks to us.

Sometimes God speaks to us in a very specific way. God spoke to me very clearly about my father after he died on January 21, 1981. I had become a Christian seven years earlier and my parents' initial reaction was one of complete horror. Gradually, over the years, they began to see a change in me. My mother became a committed Christian long before she died. My father was a man of few words. Initially, he was very unsure about my involvement in the Christian faith. By degrees, he started to become warmer about it. His death was quite sudden. What I found hardest about his death was that I wasn't sure whether he was a Christian or not.

Exactly ten days after his death, I was reading the Bible. I had asked God to speak to me about my father that day because I was still worrying about him. I happened to be reading Romans and I came across the verse, "Everyone who calls on the name of the Lord will be saved" (Romans 10:13). I sensed at that moment God was saying to me that this verse was for my father; that he had called on the name of the Lord and been saved. About five minutes later my wife, Pippa, came in and said to me, "I have been reading a verse in Acts 2:21 and I think this verse is for your father. It says, 'And everyone who calls on the name of the Lord will be saved.'" It was quite extraordinary, because that verse only appears twice in the New Testament and God had spoken to both of us through the same words at the same time in different parts of the Bible.

As God speaks to us ... we learn to hear His voice.

Three days later, we went to a Bible study in a friend's home and the Bible study was on Romans 10:13, that same passage. So three times during those three days God spoke to me about my father through the same words. Nevertheless, on my way to work I was still thinking about my father and worrying about him. As I came out of the subway, I looked up and there was a huge poster saying, "Everyone who calls upon the name of the Lord will be saved" (Romans 10:13). I remember talking to a friend about what had happened and he said, "Do you think the Lord may be trying to speak to you?"

As God speaks to us and we learn to hear His voice, our relationship with Him grows, and our love for Him deepens.

HOW DO WE HEAR GOD SPEAK THROUGH THE BIBLE?

Time is our most valuable possession. The pressure on time tends to increase as life goes on and we become busier and busier. There is a saying that "money is power, but time is life." If we are going to set aside time to read the Bible, we have to plan ahead. If we don't plan it, we will never do it. Don't be depressed if you only keep to eighty percent of your plan. Sometimes we oversleep!

It is wise to start with a realistic goal. Don't be overambitious. It is better to spend a few minutes every day than to spend an hour-and-a-half the first day and then to give up. If you have never studied the Bible before, you might like to set aside seven minutes every day. I am sure that if you do that regularly you will steadily increase it. The more you hear God's Word, the more you will want to hear it.

Mark tells us that Jesus got up early and went off to a solitary place to pray (Mark 1:35). It is important to try to find somewhere where we can be on our own. I love to go outside if I am in the country. In London it is harder to find "a solitary place." I have a corner of a room where I go to read the Bible and pray. I find that first thing in the morning is the best time, before the children are up and the telephone starts ringing. I take a cup of hot chocolate (to wake me up), the Bible, my calendar and a notebook. I use the notebook to write down prayers and also things I think God may be saying to me. I use the calendar as an aid to praying about each stage of my day, and also for jotting down things that come to my mind. This prevents them acting as a distracting thought.

Start by asking God to speak to you through the passage you are reading. Then read the passage. If you are a beginner I suggest reading a few verses of one of the Gospels each day. You might find it a help to use Bible reading notes, which are available at most Christian bookstores.

As you read ask yourself three questions:

1. What does the passage say? Read it at least once and, if necessary, compare different translations.

2. What does it mean? What did it mean to the person who first wrote it and those who first read it? This is where commentaries may be helpful.

3. How does it apply to me, my family, my work, my neighbors, the society around me? This is the most important stage. It is when we see the relevance to our own lives that Bible reading becomes so

exciting and we become conscious that we are hearing God's voice.

Finally, we must put into practice what we hear from God. Jesus said, "Therefore everyone who hears these words of mine and puts them into practice is like a wise man who built his house on the rock" (Matthew 7:24). As the nineteenth-century preacher D. L. Moody pointed out, "The Bible was not given to increase our knowledge. It was given to change lives."

Bible reading becomes so exciting.

I want to end by looking again at Psalm 1, with which we began this chapter. The psalmist encourages us to delight in the Word of God. If we do so, certain things will happen in our lives.

First, we shall *produce fruit*. The psalmist says, "He is like a tree planted by streams of water, which yields its fruit in season" (vs. 3). This promise is that our life will produce fruit—the fruit of the Spirit (as we have seen in Chapter 4). And it will produce fruit in terms of other people's lives being changed as a result. It is not only for our benefit that we read the Bible, but so that we can be a blessing to other people—to our friends, colleagues, neighbors, and the society in which we live. This is fruit that will last into eternity (John 15:16).

Secondly, we shall have strength to *persevere* in our walk with the Lord. The promise to the person whose delight is in the law of the Lord is that he will be like a tree whose "leaf does not wither" (vs. 3).

If we stay close to Jesus Christ through His Word, we will not dry up or lose our spiritual vitality. It is not enough to have great spiritual experiences, although they are very important and very wonderful. Unless we are deeply rooted in Jesus Christ, in His Word and in that relationship with Him, we won't be able to withstand the storms of life. If we *are* rooted in that relationship, if we *are* delighting in His Word, then when the storms come we shall stand.

Thirdly, the psalmist says that the person who delights in the Word of God will *prosper* in "whatever he does" (Psalm 1:3). Our lives may not be ones of material prosperity, but we shall prosper in ways that really matter in life—in our relationship with God, in our relationships with other people, and in the transforming of our characters into the likeness of Jesus Christ. These things are far more valuable than material wealth.

I hope that you will, with the psalmist and with millions of other Christians, determine to make the Bible your delight.

6 Why and How Do I Pray?

According to a Gallup poll, ninety percent of Americans say that they pray. Before I became a Christian I prayed two different types of prayers. First, I prayed a prayer taught me as a child by my grandmother (who was not herself a churchgoer), "God bless Mummy and Daddy … and everybody and make me a good boy. Amen." There was nothing wrong with the prayer, but for me it was only a formula I prayed every night before I went to sleep, with superstitious fears about what might go wrong if I didn't.

Secondly, I prayed in time of crisis. For example, at the age of seventeen, before I was a Christian, I was traveling by myself in the United States. The bus company managed to lose my backpack, which contained my clothes, money, and address book. I was left with virtually nothing. I spent ten days living in a hippie colony in Key West, Florida sharing a tent with an alcoholic. After that, with a feeling of mounting loneliness and desperation, I spent the days wandering around various American cities and the nights on the bus. One day as I walked along the street, I cried out to God (in whom I did not believe) and prayed that I would meet someone I knew. Not long afterwards, I got on the bus at 6:00 A.M. in Phoenix, Arizona, and there I saw an old school friend. He lent me some money and we traveled together for a few days. It made all the difference. I did not see it as an answer to prayer; only as a coincidence. Since becoming a Christian I have found that it is remarkable how many coincidences happen when we pray.

WHAT IS PRAYER?

Prayer is the most important activity of our lives. It is the main way in which we develop a relationship with our Father in heaven. Jesus said, "When you pray, go into your room, close the door and pray to your Father, who is unseen" (Matthew 6:6). It is a relationship rather than a ritual. It is not a torrent of mechanical and mindless words. Jesus said, "Do not keep on babbling like pagans" (Matthew 6:7). It is a conversation with our Father in heaven; a vertical conversation, not a horizontal one. A little boy once yelled, "Please, God, bring me a big box of chocolates for my birthday." His mother answered, "There is no need to shout, dear! God isn't deaf." Back came the reply, "No, but Grandpa is, and he is in the next room!" When we pray, it is not to others, or to ourselves, but to God. So prayer is a matter of relationships, and when we pray the whole Trinity is involved.

Christian prayer is prayer "to your Father"

Jesus taught us to pray, "Our Father in heaven" (Matthew 6:9). God is personal. Of course He is "beyond personality," as C. S. Lewis put it, but He is nevertheless personal. Man is made in the image of God. Personhood is a reflection of something within the nature of God. He is our loving Father; we have the extraordinary privilege of being able to come into His presence and call Him "Abba." This is an Aramaic word for which the nearest translation is "Daddy" or "Dear Father." There is a remarkable intimacy about our relationship with God and about praying to our Father in heaven.

He is not only "our Father," He is "our Father in heaven." He has heavenly power. When we pray we are speaking to the Creator of the universe. On August 20, 1977, Voyager II, the interplanetary probe launched to observe and transmit to earth data about the outer planetary system, set off from earth traveling faster than the speed of a bullet (ninety thousand miles per hour). On August 28, 1989 it reached planet Neptune, 2,700 million miles from the earth. Voyager II then left the solar system. It will not come within one light year of any star for 958,000 years. In our galaxy there are one hundred million stars like our sun. Our galaxy is one of a hundred million galaxies. In a throwaway line in Genesis, the writer tells us, "He also made the stars" (Genesis 1:16). Such is His power. Andrew Murray, the Christian writer, once said, "The power of prayer depends almost entirely upon our apprehension of who it is with whom we speak."

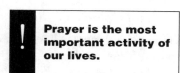

Prayer is the most important activity of our lives.

When we pray, we are speaking to a God who is both transcendent and immanent. He is far greater and more powerful than the universe He created, and yet He is there with us when we pray.

Christian prayer is through the Son

Paul says that "through him (Jesus) we both (Jews and Gentiles) have access to the Father by one Spirit" (Ephesians 2:18). Jesus said that His Father would give "whatever you ask in my name" (John 15:16). We have no right in ourselves to come to God but we are able to do so through Jesus and in His name. That is why it is customary to end prayers with "through Jesus Christ our Lord" or "in the name of Jesus." This is not just a formula; it is our acknowledgement of the fact that we can only come to God through Jesus.

It is Jesus, through His death on the cross, who removed the barrier between us and God. He is our great High Priest. That is why there is such power in the name of Jesus.

The value of a check depends not only on the amount, but also on the name that appears at the bottom. If I write out a check for ten million dollars it would be worthless; but if Bill Gates, reputed to be one of the richest men in the world, were to write a check for ten million dollars it would be worth exactly that. When we go to the bank of heaven, we have nothing deposited there. If I go in my own name, I can achieve nothing; but Jesus Christ has unlimited credit in heaven. He has given us the privilege of using His name.

Christian prayer is prayer by one Spirit (Ephesians 2:18)

We find it hard to pray, but God has not left us alone. He has given us His Spirit to live within us and help us to pray. Paul writes, "In the same way, the Spirit helps us in our weakness. We do not know what we ought to pray for, but the Spirit himself intercedes for us with groans that words cannot express. And he who searches our hearts knows the mind of the Spirit, because the Spirit intercedes for the saints in accordance with God's will" (Romans 8:26, 27). In a later chapter we shall look in more detail at the work of the Spirit. Here, it is sufficient to note that when we pray, God is praying through us by His Spirit who lives in us as Christians.

WHY PRAY?

Prayer is a vital activity. We pray for many reasons.

In the first place, prayer is the way in which we develop a relationship with our Father in heaven. Sometimes people say, "God knows our needs, so why do we have to ask?" Well, it would not be much of a relationship if there was no communication. Asking is not the only way in which we communicate with God. There are other forms of prayer: thanksgiving, praise, adoration, confession, listening, etc. But asking is an important part. As we ask God for things and see our prayers answered, our relationship with Him grows.

Next, Jesus prayed and taught us to do the same. Jesus had an uninterrupted relationship with His Father. His life was one of constant prayer. There are numerous references to His praying (for instance, Mark 1:35; Luke 6:12). He assumed His disciples would pray. He said, "When you pray" (Matthew 6:7) not, "If you pray."

Then again, if we need any further incentive, Jesus taught us that there are rewards for prayer (Matthew 6:6).

The hidden rewards of prayer are too many to enumerate. In the words of the apostle Paul, when we cry, "Abba, Father," the Holy Spirit witnesses with our spirit that we are indeed God's children, and we are granted a strong assurance of His fatherhood and love. He lifts the light of His face upon us and gives us His peace. He refreshes our soul, satisfies our hunger, quenches our thirst. We know we are no longer orphans for the Father has adopted us; no longer prodigals for we have been forgiven; no longer alienated, for we have come home.[31]

Finally, prayer not only changes us, but it also changes situations. Many people can accept that prayer will have a beneficial effect on themselves, but some have philosophical objections to the concept that prayer can change events and third parties. Rabbi Daniel Cohn-Scherbok of Kent University once wrote an article arguing that, since God already knows the future, it therefore must be predetermined. To this Clifford Longley, the religious affairs correspondent of *The Times* in London, correctly replied, "If God lives in the eternal present, He hears all prayers simultaneously. Therefore He can appropriate a prayer from next week, and attach it to an event a month ago. Prayers said after the event can be heard before they are spoken and taken into account before the event." In other words, God has all eternity to answer the split-second prayer of a driver who is about to crash.

"If God lives in the eternal present, He hears all prayers simultaneously."

On numerous occasions Jesus encouraged us to ask. He said, "Ask and it will be given to you; seek and you will find; knock and the door will be opened to you. For everyone who asks receives; he who seeks finds; and to him who knocks, the door will be opened" (Matthew 7:7, 8).

Every Christian knows, through experience, that God answers prayer. It is not possible to prove Christianity on the basis of answers to prayer because answers can always be explained away by cynics as coincidences. But the cumulative effect of answered prayer reinforces our faith in God. I keep a prayer diary and it is fascinating to me to see how day after day, week after week, year after year, God has answered my prayers.

DOES GOD ALWAYS ANSWER PRAYER?

In the passage I have cited from Matthew 7:7, 8 and in many other New Testament passages, the promises appear to be absolute.

However, when we look at the whole of Scripture, we see there are good reasons why we may not always get what we ask for.

Unconfessed sin causes a barrier between us and God: "Surely the arm of the Lord is not too short to save, nor his ear too dull to hear. But your iniquities have separated you from your God; your sins have hidden his face from you, so that he will not hear" (Isaiah 59:1, 2). God never promises to answer the prayer of a person who is not in a relationship with Him. He may graciously answer the prayer of an unbeliever (as He did in the example I gave at the beginning of the chapter), but we have no right to expect it. When people say, "I don't feel I am getting through to God. I don't feel there is anyone there," the first question to ask is whether they have ever received God's forgiveness through Christ on the cross. The barrier must be removed before we can expect God to answer our prayers.

Even as Christians our friendship with God can be marred by sin or disobedience. John writes, "Dear friends, if our hearts do not condemn us, we have confidence before God and receive from him anything we ask, because we obey his commands and do what pleases him" (1 John 3:21, 22). If we are conscious of any sin or disobedience towards God, we need to confess it and turn from it so that our friendship with God can be restored and we can approach Him again with confidence.

Our motivation can also be a hindrance to getting what we ask for. Not every request for a new Porsche gets answered! James, the brother of Jesus, writes:

"You want something but don't get it. You kill and covet, but you cannot have what you want. You quarrel and fight. You do not have, because you do not ask God. When you ask, you do not receive, because you ask with wrong motives, that you may spend what you get on your pleasures" (James 4:2, 3).

A famous example of a prayer riddled with wrong motives is that of John Ward of Hackney, written in the eighteenth century:

> O Lord, thou knowest that I have nine estates in the City of London, and likewise that I have lately purchased one estate in fee simple in the county of Essex; I beseech thee to preserve the two counties of Essex and Middlesex from fire and earthquake; and as I have a mortgage in Hertfordshire, I beg of thee likewise to have an eye of compassion on that county; and for the rest of the counties thou mayest deal with them as thou art pleased.
>
> O Lord, enable the bank to answer their bills, and make all my debtors good men. Give a prosperous voyage and return to the Mermaid ship, because I have insured it; and as thou hast said that the days of the wicked are but short, I trust in thee, that thou wilt not forget thy promise, as I have purchased an estate in reversion which will be mine on the death of that profligate young man, Sir J. L.
>
> Keep my friends from sinking, and preserve me from thieves and house breakers, and make all my servants so honest and faithful that they may attend to my interests, and never cheat me out of my property, night or day.

Sometimes prayers are not answered because what we are requesting is not good for us. God only promises to give us "good gifts'"(Matthew 7:11). He loves us and knows what is best for us. A good human father does not always give his children what they ask for. If a five-year-old wants to play with a carving knife, hopefully a good father will say "No!" God will answer "no" if the things we ask for are "either not good in themselves, or not good for us or for others, directly or indirectly, immediately or ultimately," as John Stott has written.

The answer to our prayer will either be "yes," "no," or sometimes "wait," and for this we should be extremely grateful. If we were given carte blanche we would never dare pray again. As the preacher Martyn Lloyd-Jones put it, "I thank God that He is not prepared to do anything that I may chance to ask Him ... I am profoundly grateful to God that He did not grant me certain things for which I asked, and that He shut certain doors in my face."[32] Any Christian who has been a Christian for some time will appreciate this sentiment. Ruth Graham (married to Billy Graham) told an audience in Minneapolis, "God has not always answered my prayers. If He had, I would have married the wrong man—several times." Sometimes we will not know during this life why the answer was "no."

That is why the promises in the Bible that prayers will be answered are sometimes qualified. For example, John writes, "If we ask anything *according to his will*, he hears us" (1 John 5:14, italics mine). The more we get to know God, the better we will know His will and the more our prayers will be answered.

HOW SHOULD WE PRAY?

There is no set way to pray. Prayer is an integral part of our relationship with God and therefore we are free to talk to Him as we wish. God does not want us to repeat meaningless words; He wants to hear what is on our hearts. Having said that, many people find it helpful to have a pattern for prayer. For some years I used the mnemonic ACTS.

A—Adoration: praising God for who He is and what He has done.
C—Confession: asking God's forgiveness for anything that we have done wrong.
T —Thanksgiving: for health, family, friends, etc.
S —Supplication: praying for ourselves, for our friends, and for others.

More recently I have found that I often follow the pattern from the Lord's Prayer (Matthew 6:9-13):

"Our Father in heaven" (vs. 9)

We have already looked earlier in the chapter at what this phrase means. Under this heading, I spend time thanking God for who He is and for my relationship with Him and for the ways in which He has answered prayers."

"Hallowed be your name" (vs. 9)

In Hebrew someone's name signified a revelation of that person's character. To pray that God's name be hallowed is to pray that He will be honored. So often we look around our society and see that God's name is dishonored. Many people pay no attention to Him or His laws. We should start by praying that God's name is honored in our own lives, in our church, and in the society around us.

"Your kingdom come" (vs. 10)

God's kingdom is His rule and reign. That will be complete when Jesus comes again. But this kingdom broke into history when Jesus came for the first time. Jesus demonstrated this presence of God's kingdom in His own ministry. When we pray, "Your kingdom come," we are praying for God's rule and reign to come both in the future and in the present. It includes praying for people to be converted, healed, set free from evil, filled with the Spirit, and given the gifts of the Spirit, in order that we may together serve and obey the King.

I am told that D. L. Moody wrote down a list of a hundred people and prayed for them to be converted in his lifetime. Ninety-six of them were converted by the time he died and the other four were converted at his funeral.

One Christian mother was having problems with her rebellious teenage son. He was lazy, bad-tempered, a cheat, a liar, and a thief. Later on, though outwardly respected as a lawyer, his life was dominated by worldly ambition and a desire to make money. His morals were loose. He lived with several different women and had a son by one of them. At one stage he joined a weird religious sect and adopted all kinds of strange practices. Throughout this time his mother continued to pray for him. One day, the Lord gave her a vision and she wept as she prayed, because she saw the light of Jesus Christ in her son and his face transformed. She had to wait another nine years before her son gave his life to Jesus Christ at the age of thirty-two. That man's name was Augustine. He went on to become one of the greatest theologians in the church. He always attributed his conversion to the prayers of his mother.

"Your will be done on earth as it is in heaven" (vs. 10)

This is not resignation, it is a releasing of the burdens that we so often carry. Many people are worried about decisions they face. The decisions may be about major or minor issues, but if we want to be sure that we don't make a mistake we need to pray, "Your will be done." The psalmist says, "Commit your way to the Lord; trust in him and he will act" (Psalm 37:5, *Revised Standard Version*). For example, if you are praying about whether a relationship is right, you might pray, "If this relationship is wrong, I pray that You stop it. If it is right I pray that nothing will stop it." Then, having committed it to the Lord, you can trust Him and wait for Him to act. (We will look at this subject in more detail in the next chapter; the principles in that chapter need to be taken into account.)

"Give us today our daily bread" (vs. 11)

Some have suggested that Jesus meant the spiritual bread of Holy Communion or the Bible. This is possible, but I believe the reformers were right to say that Jesus is referring here to our basic needs. Luther said it indicated "everything necessary for the preservation of this life, like food, a healthy body, good weather, house, home, wife, children, good government and peace." God is concerned about everything that you and I are concerned about. Just as I want my children to talk to me about anything they are worried about, so God wants to hear about the things we are concerned about.

A friend of mine asked a new Christian how her small business was going. She replied that it was not going very well. So my friend offered to pray for it. The new Christian replied, "I didn't know that was allowed." My friend explained that it was. They prayed, and the following week the business improved considerably. The Lord's Prayer teaches us that it is not wrong to pray about our own concerns, provided that God's name, God's kingdom and God's will are our first priority.

God wants to hear about the things we are concerned about.

"Forgive us our debts, as we also have forgiven our debtors" (vs. 12)

Jesus taught us to pray for God to forgive us our debts (that is, the things that we do wrong). Some say, "Why do we need to pray for forgiveness? Surely when we come to the Cross we are already forgiven for everything, past, present, and future?" It is true, as we have seen

> **!** **A measure of cleansing may be necessary every day.**

in the chapter on why Jesus died, that we are totally forgiven for everything, past, present, and future because Jesus took all our sins on Himself on the Cross. Yet Jesus tells us to pray, "Forgive us our debts." I find the most helpful analogy is the one given by Jesus in John 13 when Jesus moves to wash Peter's feet. Peter said, "No, you shall never wash my feet." Jesus answered, "Unless I wash you, you have no part with me." Peter replied, in effect, "Well, in that case wash my whole body." Jesus said, "A person who has had a bath needs only to wash his feet; his whole body is clean." This is a picture of forgiveness. When we come to the Cross, we are made totally clean and we are forgiven; everything is dealt with. But as we go through the world, we do things that tarnish our friendship with God. Our relationship is always secure, but our friendship is sullied with the dirt that we pick up. Each day we need to pray, "Lord forgive us, cleanse us from the dirt." We don't need to have a bath again, Jesus has done that for us, but a measure of cleansing may be necessary every day.

Jesus went on to say, "If you forgive men when they sin against you, your heavenly Father will also forgive you. But if you do not forgive men their sins, your Father will not forgive your sins" (Matthew 6:14, 15). This does not mean that by forgiving people we can earn forgiveness. We can never earn forgiveness. Jesus achieved that for us on the cross. But the sign that we are forgiven is that we are willing to forgive others. If we are not willing to forgive other people, that is evidence that we do not know forgiveness ourselves. If we really know God's forgiveness, we cannot refuse forgiveness to someone else.

"And lead us not into temptation, but deliver us from the evil one" (vs. 13)

God does not tempt us (James 1:13), but He is in control of how much we are exposed to the devil (for instance, see Job 1–2). Every Christian has a weak area, be it fear, selfish ambition, greed, pride, lust, gossiping, cynicism, or something else. If we know our weaknesses, we can pray for protection against them, as well, of course, as taking action to avoid unnecessary temptation. We will consider this whole issue in Chapter 10.

WHEN SHOULD WE PRAY?

The New Testament exhorts us to pray "always" (1 Thessalonians 5:17; Ephesians 6:18).

We do not have to be in a special building in order to pray. We can pray on the train, on the bus, in the car, on a bike, along the road, in bed, in the middle of the night, whenever and wherever we are. As in a relationship such as marriage, we can continue an ongoing conversation. Nevertheless, as in marriage, it is helpful to have time together when you know you are meeting simply to talk. Jesus said, "When you pray, go into your room, close the door and pray to your Father, who is unseen" (Matthew 6:6). He Himself went off to a solitary place in order to pray (Mark 1:35). I find it helpful to combine Bible reading and prayer at the beginning of the day, when my mind is most active. It is good to have a regular pattern. What time of day we choose will depend on our circumstances and our own particular makeup.

As well as praying alone, it is important to pray with other people. This could be in a small group of two or three, for example. Jesus said, "I tell you that if two of you on earth agree about anything you ask for, it will be done for you by my Father in heaven" (Matthew 18:19). It can be very hard praying aloud in front of other people. I remember the first time I did this, about two months after I had come to Christ. I was with two of my closest friends and we decided that we would spend some time praying together. We only prayed for about ten minutes, but when I took my shirt off afterwards it was wringing wet! Nevertheless, it is worth persevering since there is great power in praying together (Acts 12:5).

Prayer is at the heart of Christianity, because at the heart of Christianity is a relationship with God. That is why it is the most important activity of our lives. As the saying goes:

Satan laughs at our words.
Mocks at our toil.
But trembles when we pray.

7 How Does God Guide Us?

We all have to make decisions in life. We are faced with decisions about relationships, marriage, children, use of time, jobs, homes, money, holidays, possessions, giving, and so on. Some of these are very big decisions, some smaller. In many cases, it is of the utmost importance that we make the right decisions—for instance in our

choice of a marriage partner. We need God's help.

Guidance springs out of our relationship with God. He promises to guide those who are walking with Him. He says, "I will instruct you and teach you in the way you should go" (Psalm 32:8). Jesus promises to lead and guide His followers: "He calls his own sheep by name and leads them out ... His sheep follow him because they know his voice" (John 10:3, 4). He longs for us to discover His will (Colossians 1:9;

Ephesians 5:17). He is concerned about each of us as individuals. He loves us and wants to speak to us about what we should be doing with our lives—about little things as well as big things.

God has a plan for our lives (Ephesians 2:10). Sometimes people are worried by this. They think, "I'm not sure that I want God's plan for my life. Will God's plans be good?" We need not fear. God loves us and wants the very best for our lives. Paul tells us that God's will for our lives is "good, pleasing and perfect"(Romans 12:2). He said to His people through the prophet Jeremiah, "'For I know the plans I have for you,' declares the Lord, 'plans to prosper you and not to harm you, plans to give you hope and a future'" (Jeremiah 29:11).

God is saying, "Don't you realize that I have a really good plan for your life? I have prepared something wonderful." This cry from the Lord's heart came because He saw the mess His people had gotten themselves into when they didn't follow His plans. All around us we see people whose lives are in a muddle. Often people say to me after they have come to Christ, "I wish I had become a Christian five or ten years earlier. Look at my life now. It is such a mess."

All around us we see people whose lives are in a muddle.

If we are to find out about God's plans for us, we need to ask Him about them. God warned His people about embarking on plans without consulting Him: "'Woe to the obstinate children,' declares the Lord, 'to those who carry out plans that are not mine ... who go down to Egypt *without consulting me*'" (Isaiah 30:1, 2, italics mine). Of course, Jesus is the supreme example of doing the will of His Father. He was consistently "led by the Spirit" (Luke 4:1) and only did what He saw His Father doing (John 5:19).

We make mistakes because we fail to consult the Lord. We make some plan and think, "I want to do that, but I am not quite sure whether God wants me to do it. I think I'd better not ask Him, just in case it's not His will for me!"

God guides us when we are prepared to do His will rather than insisting that our own way is right. The psalmist says, "He guides the humble" (Psalm 25:9) and "confides in those who fear [respect]

> **God guides us when we are prepared to do His will.**

him" (vs. 14). God guides those whose attitude is like Mary's: "I am the Lord's servant, and I am willing to do whatever he wants" (Luke 1:38, *The Living Bible*). The moment we are prepared to do His will, He begins to reveal His plans for our lives.

I go back to a verse in the Psalms time and time again: "Commit your way to the Lord; trust in him, and he will act" (Psalm 37:5, *Revised Standard Version*). Our part is to commit the decision to the Lord and then to trust Him. When we have done that, we can wait expectantly for Him to act.

Towards the end of our time in college, one of my friends called Nicky, who had become a Christian about the same time that I did, began to get to know very well a girl who was not a Christian. He felt it was not right to marry her unless she shared his faith in Christ. He did not want to put her under any pressure. So he did what the psalmist said and committed it to the Lord. He said, in effect, "Lord, if this relationship is not right, I pray that You will stop it. If it is right, then I pray she will become a Christian by the last day of the spring term." He did not tell her or anyone else about this date. He put his trust in God and waited for Him to act. The final day of the spring term arrived, and they went a party together that night. Just before midnight she told him she wanted to go for a drive. So they got into the car and she gave him a whole string of directions out of the top of her head, just for fun: "Three left turns, three right turns, drive straight for three miles and stop." He played along and followed them. They ended up in the American cemetery, which has one enormous cross in the center surrounded by hundreds of little crosses. She was shocked and deeply moved by the symbol of the cross, and also by the fact that God had used her instructions to get her attention. She burst into tears. Moments later, she came to faith in Christ. They have now been happily married for many years and still look back and remember how God's hand was on them at that moment.

Given that we are willing to do what God wants us to do, in what ways should we expect God to speak to us? God guides us in various ways. Sometimes God speaks through one of the ways set out below; sometimes it is a combination. If it is a major decision He may speak through all of them. They are sometimes called the five "C Ss."

COMMANDING SCRIPTURE

As we have seen, God's general will for all people in all places in all circumstances is revealed in Scripture. He has told us what He thinks about a whole range of issues. From the Bible we know that certain things are wrong; we can be quite sure that God will not guide us to do these things. Sometimes a married person says, "I have fallen in love with this person. We love each other so much. I feel God is leading me to leave my spouse and to start this new relationship." But God has already made His will clear. He has said, "You shall not commit adultery" (Exodus 20:14). We can be quite sure that God will not guide us to commit adultery.

We can be quite sure that God will not guide us to commit adultery.

Sometimes people feel led to save money by not paying their income tax! But God has made it clear that we are to pay any taxes that are due (Romans 13:7). In these and many other areas God has revealed His general will. We do not need to ask His guidance; He has already given it. If we are not sure whether the Bible says anything on an issue, we may need to ask someone who knows the Bible better than we do. Once we have discovered what the Bible says, we need search no further.

Although God's general will is revealed in the Bible, we cannot always find His particular will for our lives there. As we have seen, the Bible tells us that it is His general will for people to get married. Although singleness is a high calling, it is the exception rather than the rule (see 1 Corinthians 7:2). We know that Christians are only free to marry other Christians (2 Corinthians 6:14). But the Bible does not tell us whom we should marry!

Sometimes a verse seems almost to leap off of the page at us.

As we saw in the chapter on the Bible, God still speaks today through the Scriptures. He may speak to us as we read. The psalmist says, "Your statutes ... are my counselors" (Psalm 119:24). That is not to say that we find God's will by opening the Bible anywhere at random and seeing what it says. Rather, as we develop the habit of regular, methodical Bible study we begin to find it quite extraordinary how appropriate each day's reading seems to be for the particular circumstances in which we find ourselves.

Sometimes a verse seems almost to leap off of the page at us, and we sense God speaking through it. This was certainly my experience, for example, when I sensed God calling me to change jobs. Each time I felt God speaking to me as I read the Bible, I wrote it down. I noted at least fifteen different occasions when I believe God spoke to me through the Bible about His call to me to leave my work as a lawyer and train for ordination in the Church of England.

COMPELLING SPIRIT

Guidance is very personal. When we become Christians, the Spirit of God comes to live within us. When He does so, He begins to communicate with us. We need to learn to hear His voice. Jesus said that His sheep (His followers) would recognize His voice (John 10:4, 5). We recognize a good friend's voice immediately on the telephone. If we do not know the person so well, it may be harder and take more time. The more we get to know Jesus, the easier we will find it to recognize His voice.

We find Paul and his companions, for example, planning to enter Bithynia, "but the Spirit of Jesus would not allow them to" (Acts 16:7). So they went a different way. We do not know how exactly the Spirit spoke to them, but it may have been in one of a number of ways.

Here are three examples of the way in which God speaks by His Spirit.

Often God speaks to us when we pray

Prayer is a two-way conversation. Suppose I go to the doctor and say, "Doctor, I have a number of problems: I have a problem of fungus growing under my toenails, I have hemorrhoids, my eyes itch, I need a flu shot, I have very bad backaches, and I have tennis elbow." Then, having got through my list of complaints, I look at my watch and say, "Goodness me, time is getting on. Well, I must be off. Thanks very much for listening." The doctor might want to say, "Hang on a second. Why don't you listen to me?" If whenever we pray we only speak to God and never take time to listen, we make the same mistake. In the Bible we find God speaking to His people. For example, on one occasion as the Christians were worshipping the Lord and fasting, the Holy Spirit said, "'Set apart for me Barnabas and Saul for the work to which I have called them.' So after they had fasted and prayed, they placed their hands on them and sent them off" (Acts 13:2, 3).

Again, we don't know exactly how the Holy Spirit spoke. It may be that as they were praying the thought came into their minds. That is a common way in which God speaks. People sometimes describe it as "impressions" or feeling it "in their bones." It is possible for the Holy Spirit to speak in all these ways.

Obviously such thoughts and feelings need to be tested (1 John 4:1). Is it in line with the Bible? Does it promote love? If it does not, it cannot come from a God who is love (1 John 4:16). Is it strengthening, encouraging, and comforting (1 Corinthians 14:3)? When we have made the decision, do we know God's peace (Colossians 3:15)?

God sometimes speaks to us by giving us a strong desire to do something

"God ... works in you to *will* and to act according to his good purpose" (Philippians 2:13, italics mine). As we surrender our wills to God, He works in us and often changes our desires. Again, I can speak from my own experience. Before I became a Christian, the last thing in the world I would have wanted to be was an ordained clergyman in the Church of England. Yet when I came to Christ and said I was willing to do what He wanted, I found my desires changed. Now I cannot imagine a greater privilege or a more fulfilling job for me than the one I am doing at the moment.

Sometimes people try to imagine the thing that they would least like to do and then assume that God will ask them to do exactly that. I do not believe God is like that. So don't be frightened and say, "If I become a Christian, God will make me be a missionary." If that is what He wants you to do, and your will is surrendered, He will give you a strong desire to do that.

God sometimes guides in more unusual ways

The Bible has many examples of God guiding individuals in dramatic ways. He spoke to Samuel as a small boy in a way in which he could hear with his physical ears (1 Samuel 3:4-14). He guided Abraham (Genesis 18), Joseph (Matthew 2:19), and Peter (Acts 12:7) through angels. He often spoke through prophets both in the Old Testament and in the New Testament (for instance, Agabus in Acts 11:27, 28; 21:10, 11). He guided through visions (sometimes referred to today as "pictures"). For example, one night God spoke to Paul in a vision. Paul saw a man in Macedonia standing and begging him, "Come over to Macedonia and help us." Not surprisingly, Paul and his companions took this as guidance that God had called them to preach the gospel in Macedonia (Acts 16:9, 10).

We also find examples of God guiding through dreams (for instance, Matthew 1:20; 2:12, 13, 22). I was praying for a couple who were good friends of ours. The husband had recently come to faith in Christ. The wife was highly intelligent but strongly against what had happened to her husband. She became a little hostile towards us. One night I had a dream in which I saw her face quite changed, her eyes full of the joy of the Lord. This encouraged us to continue praying and keeping close to them. A few months later she came to faith in Christ. I remember looking at her and seeing the face I had seen in the dream a few months earlier.

All these are ways in which God guided people in the past and still does today.

COMMON SENSE

When we become Christians we are not called to abandon common sense. The psalmist warns: "Do not be like the horse or the mule, which have no understanding but must be controlled by bit and bridle or they will not come to you" (Psalm 32:9). The New Testament writers often encourage us to think and never discourage us from using our minds (for instance, 2 Timothy 2:7).

If we abandon common sense, then we get ourselves into absurd situations. In his book *Knowing God,* J. I. Packer quotes an example of a woman who each morning, having consecrated the day to the Lord as soon as she woke, "would then ask him whether she was to get up or not," and would not stir till "the voice" told her to dress.

> As she put on each article she asked the Lord whether she was to put it on and very often the Lord would tell her to put on the right shoe and leave off the other; sometimes she was to put on both stockings and no shoes; and sometimes both shoes and no stockings. It was the same with all the articles of dress.[49]

It is true to say that God's promises of guidance were not given so that we could avoid the strain of thinking. Indeed, John Wesley, the father of Methodism, said that God *usually* guided him by presenting reasons to his mind for acting in a certain way. This is important in every area—especially in the areas of marriage and jobs.

Common sense is one of the factors to be taken into account in the whole area of choosing a partner for life. It is common sense to look at at least three very important areas.

Spiritual compatibility. A Christian should only marry another Christian. Paul warns of the danger of marrying someone who is not a Christian (2 Corinthians 6:14). In practice, if one of the parties is not a Christian, it nearly always leads to a great tension in the marriage. The Christian feels torn between a desire to serve his or her partner and a desire to serve the Lord. But spiritual compatibility means more than the fact that both are Christians. It means that each party respects the other's spirituality, rather than simply being able to say, "At least they pass the test of being a Christian."

Personal compatibility. Obviously, our marriage partner should be a very good friend and someone with whom there is a great deal in common. One of the many advantages of not sleeping together before getting married is that it is easier to concentrate on this area and discover whether or not there is personal compatibility. Often the sexual side can dominate the early stages of a relationship. If the foundations have not been built on friendship, then when the initial sexual excitement wears off it can leave the relationship with a very fragile basis.

Physical compatibility. By physical compatibility I mean we should be attracted to each other. It is not enough to be spiritually and emotionally compatible; the chemistry must work as well. Often the secular world puts it first, but this comes last in the order of priorities. The world often says that it is necessary to sleep together in order to see whether there is sexual compatibility. This is quite wrong. In the biological sense, any incompatibility that can be tested by sexual intercourse is so rare that it can be discounted.

Again, common sense is vital when considering God's guidance about our jobs and careers. The general rule is that we should stay with the job we are already in until God calls us to do something else (1 Corinthians 7:17-24). Having said that, in seeking God's will for one's career, it is common sense to take a long-term view of life. It is wise to look ahead ten, fifteen, twenty years and ask the questions: "Where is my present job taking me? Is that where I want to go in the long term? Or is my long-term vision for something quite different? In which case, where should I be now in order to get there?"

COUNSEL OF THE SAINTS[50]

The Book of Proverbs is full of injunctions to seek wise advice. The writer asserts that "a wise man listens to advice" (Proverbs 12:15). He warns that "plans fail for lack of counsel," but on the other hand, "with many advisers they succeed" (Proverbs 15:22). Therefore, he urges, "Make plans by seeking advice" (Proverbs 20:18).

While seeking advice is very important, we need to remember that ultimately our decisions are between us and God. They are our responsibility. We cannot shift that responsibility onto others or seek to blame them if things go wrong. The counsel of the saints is part of guidance—but it is not the only part. Sometimes it may be right to go ahead in spite of the advice of others.

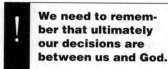

> **! We need to remember that ultimately our decisions are between us and God.**

If we are faced with a decision where we need advice, whom should we consult? To the writer of Proverbs, "fear of the Lord is the beginning of wisdom (Proverbs 9:10)." Presumably, therefore, he is thinking of advice from those who "fear the Lord." The best advisors are usually godly Christian people with wisdom and experience whom we respect. (It is also wise to seek the advice of parents whom we are to honor, even if we are past the age of being under their authority. Even if they are not Christians, they know us very well and

113

can often have important insights into situations.)

I have found it a real help throughout my Christian life to have someone who is a mature Christian whom I respect and to whom I can go for advice on a whole range of issues. This has been different people at different times. I am so grateful to God for their wisdom and help in many areas. Often God's insight has come as we talked through the issues together.

When it comes to bigger decisions, I have found it helpful to seek a range of advice. Over the question of ordination I sought the advice of my parents, my two closest friends, my pastor, and those who were involved in the official process of selection.

The people whom we ask for advice should not be chosen on the basis that they will agree with what we have already planned to do! Sometimes one sees a person consulting countless people in the hope that he or she will eventually find somebody who will endorse their plans. Such advice has little weight and simply enables the person to say, "And I consulted this person and he or she agreed."

We should consult people on the basis of their spiritual authority or their relationship to us, regardless of what we may anticipate their views to be. When my friends, Nicky and Sila Lee, who now minister in a church in central London, became Christians, they wondered whether it was right to continue their relationship, because although they were very much in love they were still so young and had no immediate prospects of marriage.

Nicky talked to a very wise Christian man for whom he had great respect. Nicky knew the man had firm views on the subject of relationships and that he felt it was unwise to be too deeply involved while still in college. Nevertheless, Nicky decided to consult him.

The man asked Nicky, "Have you committed your relationship with Sila to the Lord?" Nicky replied with some hesitation and great honesty, "I think I have, but sometimes I am not sure," to which this wise man replied, "I can see that you love her. I think you should continue in your relationship with her." Because this advice came from a surprising source it carried additional weight. The advice was very good, and they have now had many years of happily married life to prove it.

CIRCUMSTANTIAL SIGNS

God is in ultimate control of all events; the writer of Proverbs points out: "In his heart a man plans his course, but the Lord determines his steps" (Proverbs 16:9). Sometimes God opens doors (1 Corinthians 16:9,) and sometimes He closes them (Acts 16:7).

On two occasions in my life God has closed the door on something that I very much wanted, and which I believed at the time was God's will. I tried to force the doors open. I prayed and I struggled and I fought, but they would not open. On both occasions I was bitterly disappointed. But I understand now, years later, why God closed those doors. Indeed I am grateful that He did. However, I am not sure we will ever know this side of heaven why God has closed certain doors in our lives.

Sometimes God opens doors in a remarkable way. The circumstances and the timing point clearly to the hand of God (for instance, Genesis 24). Michael Bourdeaux is head of Keston College, a research unit devoted to helping believers in what were communist lands. His work and research are respected by governments all over the world. He studied Russian at Oxford and his Russian teacher, Dr. Zernov, sent him a letter he had received because he thought it would interest him. It detailed how monks were beaten up by the KGB and subjected to inhuman medical examinations; how they were being rounded up in trucks and dumped many hundreds of miles away. The letter was written very simply, with no adornment, and as he read it Michael Bourdeaux felt he was hearing the true voice of the persecuted church. The letter was signed Varavva and Pronina.

In August 1964, Michael went on a trip to Moscow, and on his first evening there met up with old friends who detailed how the persecutions were getting worse. In particular the old church of St. Peter and St. Paul had been demolished. They suggested that he go and see it for himself.

So he took a taxi and arrived at dusk. When he came to the square where he had remembered a very beautiful church, he found nothing except a twelve-foot-high fence, which hid the rubble where the church had been. Over on the other side of the square, climbing the fence to try to see what was inside, were two women. He watched them, and when they finally left the square he followed them for a hundred yards and eventually caught up with them. They asked, "Who are you?" He replied, "I am a foreigner. I have come to find out what is happening here in the Soviet Union."

They took him back to the house of another woman who asked him why he had come. He said he had received a letter from the Ukraine via Paris. When she asked who it was from, he replied, "Varavva and Pronina." There was silence. He wondered if he had said something wrong. A flood of uncontrolled sobbing followed. The woman pointed and said, "This is Varavva, and this is Pronina."

Sometimes we hear God correctly, but we get the timing wrong.

The population of Russia is over one hundred forty million. The Ukraine, from where the letter was written, is over eight hundred miles from Moscow. Michael Bourdeaux had flown from England six months after the letter had been written. He and the women would not have met had either party arrived at the demolished church an hour earlier or an hour later. That was one of the ways God called Michael Bourdeaux to set up his life's work.[33]

Don't be in a hurry

Sometimes God's guidance seems to come immediately when it is asked for (for instance, Genesis 24), but often it takes much longer—sometimes months or even years. We may have a sense that God is going to do something in our lives but have to wait a long time for the fulfillment. On these occasions we need patience like that of Abraham who "after waiting patiently ... received what was promised" (Hebrews 6:15). While waiting, he was tempted at one point to try and fulfill God's promises by his own means—with disastrous results (see Genesis 16 and 21).

Sometimes we hear God correctly, but we get the timing wrong. God spoke to Joseph in a dream about what would happen to him and his family. He probably expected immediate fulfillment, but he had to wait years. Indeed, while he was in prison it must have been hard for him to believe that his dreams would ever be fulfilled. But thirteen years after the original dream, he saw God's fulfillment. The waiting was part of the preparation (see Genesis 37–50).

In this area of guidance, we all make mistakes. Sometimes, like Abraham, we try to fulfill God's plans by our own wrong methods. Like Joseph we get the timing wrong. Sometimes we feel that we have made too much of a mess of our lives by the time we come to Christ for God to do anything with us. But God is greater than that. He is able to "restore to you the years which the swarming locust has eaten" (Joel 2:25, *Revised Standard Version*). He is able to make something good out of whatever is left of our lives—whether it is a short time or a long time—if we will offer what we have to Him and cooperate with His Spirit.

Lord Radstock was staying in a hotel in Norway in the mid-nineteenth century. He heard a little girl playing the piano down in the hallway. She was making a terrible noise: "Plink ... plunk ... plink ..." It was driving him mad! A man came and sat beside her and began playing alongside her, filling in the gaps. The result was the most beautiful music. He later discovered that the man playing alongside was the girl's father, Aleksandr Borodin, composer of the opera *Prince Igor.*

Paul writes that "in all things God works for the good of those who love him, who have been called according to his purpose" (Romans 8:28). As we falteringly play our part—seeking His will for our lives by reading (commanding Scripture), listening (controlling spirit), thinking (common sense), talking (counsel of the saints), watching (circumstantial signs), and waiting—God comes and sits alongside us "and in all things ... works for the good." He takes our plink, plunk, plink and makes something beautiful out of our lives.

8 Who Is the Holy Spirit?

I had a group of friends in college, five of whom were called Nicky! We used to meet for lunch most days. In February 1974 most of us came to faith in Jesus Christ. We immediately became very enthusiastic about our new-found faith. One of the Nickys, however, was slow to get going. He didn't seem excited about his relationship with God, with reading the Bible, or with praying.

One day, someone prayed for him to be filled with the Spirit. He was; and it transformed his life. A great big smile came across his face. He became well-known for his radiance; he still is years later. Thereafter, if there was a Bible study or a prayer meeting or a church in reach, Nicky was there. He loved to be with other Christians. He developed the most magnetic personality. People were drawn to him, and he helped many others to believe and to be filled with the Spirit in the way that he had been.

What was it that made such a difference to Nicky? I think that he would say it was the experience of the Holy Spirit. Many people know a certain amount about God the Father and Jesus the Son. But there is a great deal of ignorance about the Holy Spirit. Hence, three chapters of this book are devoted to the third person of the Trinity.

Some old translations speak of the "Holy Ghost," and this can make Him seem a little frightening. The Holy Spirit is not a ghost but a Person. He has all the characteristics of personhood. He thinks (Acts 15:28), speaks (Acts 1:16), leads (Romans 8:14), and can be grieved (Ephesians 4:30). He is sometimes described as the Spirit of Christ (Romans 8:9, or the Spirit of Jesus (Acts 16:7). He is the way in which Jesus is present with His people. The schoolchild's definition is "Jesus' other self."

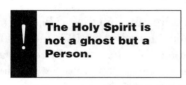

The Holy Spirit is not a ghost but a Person.

What is He like? He is sometimes described in the original Greek as the *parakletos* (John 14:16). This is a difficult word to translate. It means "one called alongside," a counselor, a comforter, and an encourager. Jesus said the Father will give you "another" counselor. The word for "another" means "of the same kind." In other words, the Holy Spirit is just like Jesus.

In this chapter I want to look at the person of the Holy Spirit: who He is and what we can learn about Him as we trace His activity through the Bible from Genesis 1 through to the Day of Pentecost. Because the Pentecostal movement began at the beginning of this century it might be tempting to think that the Holy Spirit is a twentieth-century phenomenon. This is, of course, far from the truth.

HE WAS INVOLVED IN CREATION

We see evidence of the activity of the Holy Spirit in the opening verses of the Bible: "In the beginning God created the heavens and the earth. Now the earth was formless and empty, darkness was over the surface of the deep, and the Spirit of God was hovering over the waters" (Genesis 1:1, 2).

We see in the account of the creation how the Spirit of God caused new things to come into being and brought order out of chaos. He is the same Spirit today. He often brings new things into people's lives and into churches. He brings order and peace into chaotic lives, freeing people from harmful habits and addictions and from the confusion and mess of broken relationships.

When God created man, He "formed the man from the dust of the ground and breathed into his nostrils the breath of life, and the man became a living being"(Genesis 2:7). The Hebrew word implied here for breath is *ruach*, which is also the word for "Spirit." The *ruach* of God brings physical life to man formed from dust. Likewise, He brings spiritual life to people and churches, both of which can be as dry as dust!

Some years ago I was speaking to a clergyman who was telling me that his life and his church had been like that—a bit dusty. One day he and his wife were filled with the Spirit of God, they found a new enthusiasm for the Bible, and their lives were transformed. His church became a center of life. The youth group, started by his son who had also been filled with the Spirit, experienced explosive growth and became one of the largest in the area.

Many are hungry for life and are attracted to people and churches where they see the life of the Spirit of God.

HE CAME ON PARTICULAR PEOPLE AT PARTICULAR TIMES FOR PARTICULAR TASKS

When the Spirit of God comes upon people something happens. He does not just bring a nice warm feeling! He comes for a purpose and we see examples of this in the Old Testament.

Bezalel, the Artist. The Spirit filled people for artistic work. The Spirit of God filled Bezalel "with skill, ability and knowledge in all kinds of crafts—to make artistic designs for work in gold, silver and bronze, to cut and set stones, to work in wood, and to engage in all kinds of craftsmanship" (Exodus 31:3-5).

It is possible to be a talented musician, writer, or artist without being filled with the Spirit. But when the Spirit of God fills people for these tasks their work often takes on a new dimension. It has a different effect on others. It has a far greater spiritual impact. This can be true even where the natural ability of the musician or artist is not particularly outstanding. Hearts can be touched and lives changed. No doubt something like this happened through Bezalel.

Gideon, the Leader. The Spirit also filled individuals for the task of leadership. During the time of the Judges, the people of Israel were often overrun by various foreign nations. At one time it was the Midianites. God called Gideon to lead Israel. Gideon was very conscious of his own weakness and asked, "How can I save Israel? My clan is the weakest in Manasseh, and I am the least in my family" (Judges 6:15). Yet when the Spirit of God came upon Gideon (vs. 34), he became one of the remarkable leaders of the Old Testament.

> **!** **God often uses those who feel weak, inadequate, and ill-equipped.**

In leadership, God often uses those who feel weak, inadequate, and ill-equipped. When they are filled with the Spirit, they become outstanding leaders. A notable example of this was the Reverend E. J. H. "Bash" Nash. As a nineteen-year-old clerk in an insurance office he had come to faith in Christ and was a man who was full of the Spirit of God. It has been written about him that "there was nothing particularly impressive about him ... He was neither athletic nor adventurous. He claimed no academic prowess or artistic talent."[34] Yet John Stott (whom he led to Christ) said of him: "Nondescript in outward appearance, his heart was ablaze with Christ." The obituary in the national and the church press summed up his life like this:

> Bash was a quiet, unassuming clergyman who never made the limelight, hit the headlines or wanted preferment, and yet whose influence within the Church of England during the last 50 years was probably greater than almost any of his contemporaries, for there must be hundreds of men today, many in positions of responsibility, who thank God for him for it was through his ministry that they were led to a Christian commitment.
>
> Those who knew him well, and those who worked with him, never expect to see his like again; for rarely can anyone have meant so much to so many as this quietly spoken, modest and deeply spiritual man.[35]

Samson, the Strong Man. Elsewhere we see the Holy Spirit filling people with strength and power. The story of Samson is well known. On one occasion, the Philistines tied him up by binding him with ropes. Then, "The Spirit of the Lord came upon him in power. The ropes on his arms became like charred flax, and the bindings dropped from his hands" (Judges 15:14).

What is true in the Old Testament physically is often true in the New Testament spiritually. It is not that we are physically bound by ropes, but that we are tied down by fears, habits, or addictions that grip on our lives. We are controlled by bad temper or by patterns of thought such as envy, jealousy, or lust. We know that we are bound when we cannot stop something, even when we want to. When the Spirit of God came upon Samson, the ropes became like charred flax and he was free. The Spirit of God is able to set people free today from anything that binds them.

The Spirit of God is able to set people free from anything that binds them.

Isaiah, the Prophet. Later on we see how the Spirit of God came upon the prophet Isaiah to enable him "to preach good news to the poor … to bind up the brokenhearted, to proclaim freedom for the captives and release from darkness for the prisoners" and "to comfort all who mourn" (Isaiah 61:1, 2).

We sometimes feel a sense of helplessness when confronted with the problems of the world. I often felt this before I was a Christian. I knew I had little or nothing to offer those whose lives were in a mess. I still feel like that sometimes. But I know that with the help of the Spirit of God, we do indeed have something to give. The Spirit of God enables us to bring the good news of Jesus Christ to bind up those with broken hearts; to proclaim freedom to those who are in captivity to things in their lives that deep down they hate; to release those who are imprisoned by their own wrongdoing; and to bring the comfort of the Holy Spirit (who is after all *the* Comforter) to those who are sad, grieving, or mourning. If we are going to help people in a way that lasts eternally, we cannot do so without the Spirit of God.

HE WAS PROMISED BY THE FATHER

We have seen examples of the work of the Spirit of God in the Old Testament. But His activity was limited to particular people at particular times for particular tasks. As we go through the Old Testament, we find that God promises that He will do something new. The New Testament calls this "the promise of the Father." There is an increasing sense of anticipation. *What was going to happen?*

In the Old Testament God made a covenant with His people. He said that He would be their God and that they would be His people. He required that they should keep His laws. Sadly, the people found that they were unable to keep His commands. The Old Covenant was consistently broken.

God promised that one day He would make a *New* Covenant with His people. This covenant would be different from the first covenant: "I will put my law in their minds and write it on their hearts" (Jeremiah 31:33). In other words, under the New Covenant the law would be internal rather than external. If you go on a long hike, you start off by carrying your provisions on your back. They weigh you down and slow you up. But when you have eaten them,

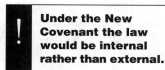

Under the New Covenant the law would be internal rather than external.

not only has the weight gone but also you have a new energy coming from inside. What God promised through Jeremiah was a time when the law would no longer be a weight on the outside but would become a source of energy from the inside. *How was this going to happen?*

Ezekiel gives us the answer. He was a prophet, and God spoke through him, elaborating on the earlier promise. "I will give you a new heart and put a new spirit in you," he said. "I will remove from you your heart of stone and give you a heart of flesh. And I will put my Spirit in you and move you to follow my decrees and be careful to keep my laws" (Ezekiel 36:26, 27).

God was saying through the prophet Ezekiel that this is what will happen when God puts His Spirit within us. This is how He will change our hearts and make them soft (hearts of flesh) rather than hard (hearts of stone). The Spirit of God will move us to follow His decrees and keep His laws.

Jackie Pullinger has spent more than twenty years working in what was the lawless walled city of Hong Kong. She has given her life to working with prostitutes, heroin addicts, and gang members. She began a memorable talk by saying, "God wants us to have soft hearts and hard feet. The trouble with many of us is that we have hard hearts and soft feet." Christians should have hard feet in that we should be tough rather than morally weak or "wet." Jackie is a glowing example of this in her willingness to go without sleep, food, and comfort in order to serve others. Yet she also has a soft heart: a heart filled with compassion. The toughness is in her feet, not her heart.

"The trouble with many of us is that we have hard hearts and soft feet."

We have seen what the promise of the Father involves and how it is going to happen. The prophet Joel tells us *to whom* it is going to happen. God says through Joel:

I will pour out my Spirit on all people,
Your sons and daughters will prophesy,
    your old men will dream dreams,
    your young men will see visions.
Even on my servants, both men and women,
    I will pour out my Spirit in those days.
        (Joel 2:28, 29)

Joel is foretelling that the promise will no longer be reserved for particular people at particular times for particular tasks, but it will be for all. God will pour out His Spirit regardless of sex ("sons and daughters … men and women"); regardless of age ("old men … young men"); regardless of background, race, color, or rank ("even on my servants"). There will be a new ability to hear God ("prophesy … dream … see visions"). Joel prophesied that the Spirit would be poured out with great generosity on all God's people.

Yet all these promises remained unfulfilled for at least three hundred years. The people waited and waited for the promise of the Father to be fulfilled until at the coming of Jesus there was a burst of activity of the Spirit of God.

With the birth of Jesus, the trumpet sounds. Almost everyone connected with the birth of Jesus was filled with the Spirit of God. John the Baptist, who was to prepare the way, was filled with the Spirit even before his birth (Luke 1:15). Mary, Jesus' mother, was promised: "The Holy Spirit will come upon you, and the power of the Most High will overshadow you" (Luke 1:35). When Elizabeth, her cousin, came into the presence of Jesus, still in his mother's womb, she too was "filled with the Holy Spirit" (vs. 41). Even John the Baptist's father Zechariah was "filled with the Holy Spirit" (vs. 67). Almost every case includes an outburst of praise or prophecy.

JOHN THE BAPTIST LINKS HIM WITH JESUS

When John was asked whether he was the Christ he replied: "I baptize you with water. But one more powerful than I will come, the thongs of whose sandals I am not worthy to untie. He will baptize you with the Holy Spirit and with fire" (Luke 3:16). Baptism with water is very important, but it is not enough. Jesus is the Spirit baptizer. The Greek word means "to overwhelm," "to immerse," or "to plunge." This is what should happen when we are baptized in the Spirit. We should be completely overwhelmed by, immersed in, and plunged into the Spirit of God.

Sometimes this experience is like a hard, dry sponge being dropped into water.

Sometimes this experience is like a hard, dry sponge being dropped into water. There can be a hardness in our lives that stops us absorbing the Spirit of God. It may take a little time for the initial hardness to wear off and for the sponge to be filled. So it is one thing for the sponge to be in the water ("baptized"), but it is another for the water to be in the sponge ("filled"). When the sponge is filled with water, the water literally pours out of it.

Jesus was a man completely filled with the Spirit of God. The Spirit of God descended on Him in bodily form at His baptism (Luke 3:22). He returned to the Jordan "full of the Holy Spirit" and was "led by the Spirit in the desert" (Luke 4:1). He returned to Galilee "in the power of the Spirit" (vs. 14). In a synagogue in Nazareth He read the lesson from Isaiah 61:1, "The Spirit of the Lord is on me" and said, "Today this scripture is fulfilled in your hearing" (vs. 21).

JESUS PREDICTED HIS PRESENCE

Feast of Tabernacles. On one occasion Jesus went to a Jewish feast called the Feast of Tabernacles. Thousands of Jews would go to Jerusalem to celebrate the feast, looking back to the time when Moses brought water from a rock. They thanked God for providing water in the past year and prayed that He would do the same in the coming year. They looked forward to a time when water would pour out of the temple (as prophesied by Ezekiel), becoming deeper and deeper and bringing life, fruitfulness, and healing wherever it went (Ezekiel 47).

This passage was read at the Feast of Tabernacles and enacted visually. The high priest would go down to the pool of Siloam and fill a golden pitcher with water. He would then lead the people to the temple, where he would pour water through a funnel in the west side of the altar, and into the ground, in anticipation of the great river that would flow from the temple. According to Rabbinic tradition, Jerusalem was the navel of the earth and the temple of Mount Zion was the center of the navel (its "belly" or "innermost being").

On the last day of the feast, Jesus stood up and proclaimed, "If anyone thirst, let him come to me and drink. He who believes in me, as the scripture has said, 'Out of his heart [the original word means "belly" or "innermost being"] shall flow rivers of living water'" (John 7:38, *Revised Standard Version*). Jesus was saying that the promises of

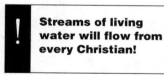

Streams of living water will flow from every Christian!

Ezekiel and others would not be fulfilled in a place, but in a person. It is out of the innermost being of Jesus that the river of life will flow. Also, in a derivative sense, the streams of living water will flow from every Christian! ("Whoever believes in me," vs. 38). From us, Jesus says, this river will flow, bringing life, fruitfulness, and healing to others promised by God through Ezekiel.

John went on to explain that Jesus was speaking about the Holy Spirit "whom those who believed in him were later to receive"

(John 7:39). He added that, "up to that time the Spirit had not been given" (vs. 39). The promise of the Father had still not been fulfilled. Even after the crucifixion and resurrection of Jesus, the Spirit was not poured out. Later, Jesus told His disciples, "I am going to send you what my Father has promised; but stay in the city until you have been clothed with power from on high" (Luke 24:49).

Power from on high. Just before He ascended to heaven Jesus again promised, "You will receive power when the Holy Spirit comes on you" (Acts 1:8). But still they had to wait and pray for another ten days. Then, at last on the Day of Pentecost: "Suddenly a sound like the blowing of a violent wind came from heaven and filled the whole house where they were sitting. They saw what seemed to be tongues of fire that separated and came to rest on each of them. All of them were filled with the Holy Spirit and began to speak in other tongues as the Spirit enabled them" (Acts 2:2-4).

It had happened. The promise of the Father had been fulfilled.

It had happened. The promise of the Father had been fulfilled. The crowd was amazed and mystified.

Peter stood up and explained what had occurred. He looked back to the promises of God in the Old Testament and explained how all their hopes and aspirations were now being fulfilled before their eyes. He explained that Jesus had "received from the Father the promised Holy Spirit" and had "poured out what you now see and hear" (Acts 2:33).

When the crowd asked what they needed to do, Peter told them to repent and be baptized in the name of Jesus so that they could receive forgiveness. Then he promised that they would receive the gift of the Holy Spirit. For, he said: "The promise is for you and your children and for *all* who are far off—for all whom the Lord our God will call" (v. 39, italics mine).

We now live in the age of the Spirit. The promise of the Father has been fulfilled. Every single Christian receives the promise of the Father. It is no longer just for particular people, at particular times for particular tasks. It is for *all* Christians, including you and me.

9 What Does the Holy Spirit Do?

> Jesus answered, "I tell you the truth, no one can enter the kingdom of God unless he is born of water and the Spirit. Flesh gives birth to flesh, but the Spirit gives birth to spirit. You should not be surprised at my saying, 'You must be born again.' The wind blows wherever it pleases. You hear its sound, but you cannot tell where it comes from or where it is going. So it is with everyone born of the Spirit" (John 3:5-8).

A couple of years ago I was in a church in Brighton. One of the Sunday school teachers was telling us about her Sunday school class the previous week. She had been telling the children about Jesus' teaching on being born again in John 3:5-8. She was trying to explain to the children about the difference between physical birth and spiritual birth. In trying to draw them out on the subject she asked, "Are you born a Christian?" One little boy replied, "No, Miss. You are born normal!"

The expression "born again" has become a cliché. It was popularized in the United States and has been used even to advertise cars. Actually, Jesus was the first person to use the expression of people who were "born of the Spirit" (John 3:8).

A new baby is born as a result of a man and a woman coming together in sexual intercourse. In the spiritual realm, when the Spirit of God and the spirit of a man or woman come together, a new spiritual being is created. There is a new birth, spiritually. This is what Jesus is speaking about when He says, "You must be born again."

Jesus was saying that physical birth is not enough. We need to be born again by the Spirit. This is what happens when we become Christians. Every single Christian is born again. We may not be able to put a finger on the exact moment it occurred, but just as we know we are alive physically, so we should know we are alive spiritually.

When we are born physically, we are born into a family. When we are born again spiritually, we are born into a Christian family. Much of the work of the Spirit can be seen in terms of a family. He assures us of our relationship with our Father and helps us to develop that relationship. He produces in us a family likeness. He unites us with our brothers and sisters, giving each member of the family different gifts and abilities. And He enables the family to grow in size.

In this chapter, we will look at each of these aspects of the Spirit's work in us as Christians. Until we become Christians, the Spirit's work is primarily to convict us of our sin and our need for Jesus Christ, to convince us of the truth, and to enable us to put our faith in Him (John 16:7-15).

SONS AND DAUGHTERS OF GOD

The moment we come to Christ we receive complete forgiveness. The barrier between us and God has been removed. Paul says, "There is now no condemnation for those who are in Christ Jesus" (Romans 8:1). Jesus took all our sins—past, present, and future. God takes all our sins and buries them in the depths of the sea (Micah 7:19). As the Dutch author Corrie Ten Boom used to say, "He puts up a sign saying 'No fishing.'"

Not only does the Spirit wipe the slate clean, but He also brings us into a relationship with God as sons and daughters. Not all men and women are children of God in this sense, although all of us were created by God. It is only to those who receive Jesus, to those who believe in His name, that He gives the "right to become children of God" (John 1:12). Sonship in the New Testament (which is used in the generic sense to include sons and daughters) is not a natural status, but a spiritual one. We become sons and daughters of God not by being born, but by being born again by the Spirit.

The Book of Romans has been described as the Himalayas of the New Testament. Chapter 8 is Mount Everest, and verses 14-17 could well be described as the peak of Everest.

> Because those who are led by the Spirit of God are sons of God. For you did not receive a spirit that makes you a slave again to fear, but you received the Spirit of sonship. And by him we cry, "Abba, Father." The Spirit himself testifies with our spirit that we are God's children. Now if we are children, then we are heirs— heirs of God and co-heirs with Christ, if indeed we share in his sufferings in order that we may also share in his glory (Romans 8:14-17).

Highest privilege. First of all, there is no higher privilege than to be a child of God. Under Roman law, if an adult wanted an heir he

135

could either choose one of his own sons or adopt a son. God has only one begotten Son—Jesus—but He has many adopted sons. In a fairy tale a reigning monarch adopts waifs and strays and makes them princes. In Christ, the fairy tale has become solid fact. We have been adopted into God's family. There could be no higher honor.

Billy Bray was a drunken and loose-living miner from Cornwall, England, born in 1794. He was always getting involved in fights and domestic quarrels. At the age of twenty-nine he became a Christian. He went home and told his wife, "You will never see me drunk again, by the help of the Lord." She never did. His words, his tone, and his looks had magnetic power. He was charged with divine electricity. Crowds of miners would come and hear him preach. Many were converted and there were some remarkable healings. He was always praising God and saying that he had abundant reason to rejoice. He described himself as "a young prince." He was the adopted son of God, the king of kings, and therefore he was a prince, already possessing royal rights and privileges. His favorite expression was, "I am the son of a King."[36]

Once we know our status as adopted sons and daughters of God, we realize that there is no status in the world that even compares with the privilege of being a child of the Creator of the universe.

Closest intimacy. Secondly, as children we have the closest possible intimacy with God. Paul says that by the Spirit we cry, "Abba, Father!" Nowhere in the Old Testament is God addressed as *Abba*. The use of this word in addressing God was distinctive of Jesus. It is impossible to translate the Aramaic word *Abba*. The nearest equivalent translation is probably "dear Father" or "Daddy." The English word "Daddy" tends to suggest a Western pal-like relationship to a parent, whereas in Jesus' day the father was an authority figure. "Abba," although a term of great intimacy, is not a juvenile word. It was the term Jesus used in addressing God. Jesus allows us to share in that intimate relationship with God when we receive His Spirit. "For you did not receive a spirit that makes you a slave again to fear, but you received the Spirit of sonship" (Romans 8:15).

Prince Charles has many titles. He is the Heir Apparent to the Crown, His Royal Highness, the Prince of Wales, Duke of Cornwall, Knight of the Garter, Colonel in Chief of the Royal Regiment of

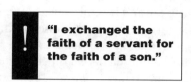

Wales, Duke of Rothesay, Knight of the Thistle, Commander of the Royal Navy, Great Master of the Order of Bath, Earl of Chester, Earl of Carrick, Baron of Renfrew, Lord of the Isles, and Great

"I exchanged the faith of a servant for the faith of a son."

Steward of Scotland. We would address him as "Your Royal Highness," but I suspect to William and Harry he is "Daddy." When we become children of God, we have an intimacy with our heavenly king. John Wesley, who had been very religious before his conversion, said about his conversion, "I exchanged the faith of a servant for the faith of a son."

Deepest experience. Thirdly, the Spirit gives us the deepest possible experience of God. "The Spirit himself testifies with our spirit that we are God's children" (Romans 8:16). He wants us to know, deep within, that we are children of God. In the same way that I want my children to know and experience my love for them and my relationship with them, so God wants His children to be assured of that love and of that relationship.

One man who only experienced this quite late in his life is the South African Bishop Bill Burnett, who was at one time Archbishop of Capetown. I heard him say, "When I became a bishop I believed in theology [the truth about God], but not in God. I was a practical atheist. I sought righteousness by doing good." One day, after he had been a bishop for fifteen years, he went to speak at a confirmation service on the text in Romans, "God has poured out his love [that is, his love for us] into our hearts by the Holy Spirit, whom he has given us" (Romans 5:5). After he had preached, he came home, poured himself a strong drink, and was reading the paper when he felt the Lord saying, "Go and pray." He went into his chapel, knelt down in silence and sensed the Lord saying to him, "I want your body." He could not quite understand why (he is tall and thin and says, "I'm not exactly Mr. Universe"). However, he gave every part of himself to the Lord. "Then," he said, "what I preached about happened. I experienced electric shocks of love." He found himself flat on the floor and heard the Lord saying, "You are my son." When he got up, he knew indeed that something had happened. It proved a turning point in his life and ministry. Since then, through his ministry many others have come to experience sonship through the witness of the Spirit.

Greatest security. Fourthly, Paul tells us that to be a son or daughter of God is the greatest security. For if we are children of God we are also "heirs of God and co-heirs with Christ" (Romans 8:17). Under Roman law an adopted son would take his father's name and inherit his estate. As children of God we are heirs. The only difference is that we

To be a son or daughter of God is the greatest security.

inherit not on the death of our father, but on our own death. This is why Billy Bray was thrilled to think that "his heavenly Father had reserved everlasting glory and blessedness" for him. We will enjoy an eternity of love with Jesus.

Paul adds, "If indeed we share in his sufferings in order that we may also share in his glory" (vs. 17). This is not a condition but an observation. Christians identify with Jesus Christ. This may mean some rejection and opposition here and now, but that is nothing compared to our inheritance as children of God.

DEVELOPING THE RELATIONSHIP

Birth is not just the climax of a period of gestation; it is the beginning of a new life and new relationships. Our relationship with our parents grows and deepens over a long period. This happens as we spend time with them; it does not happen overnight.

Our relationship with God, as we have seen in the early chapters, grows and deepens as we spend time with Him. The Spirit of God helps us to develop our relationship with God. He brings us into the presence of the Father. "For through him [Jesus] we both [Jews and Gentiles alike] have access to the Father by one Spirit" (Ephesians 2:18). Through Jesus, by the Spirit, we have access to the presence of God.

Jesus, through His death on the cross, removed the barrier between us and God. That is why we are able to come into God's presence. Often we don't appreciate that when we are praying.

When I was in college I had a room above Barclay's Bank on High Street. We used to have regular lunch parties in this room. One day we were discussing whether or not the noise we made could be heard in the bank below. In order to find out, we decided to conduct an experiment. A young woman called Kay went down into the bank. As it was lunchtime, the bank was packed with customers. The arrangement was that we would gradually build up the noise. First, one of us would jump on the floor, then two, three, four, and eventually five. Next we would jump off chairs and then off the table. We wanted to see at which point we could be heard downstairs in the bank.

It turned out that the ceiling was thinner than we had thought. The first jump could definitely be heard. The second made a loud noise. After about the fifth, which sounded like a thunderstorm, there was total silence in the bank. Everyone had stopped cashing checks and was looking at the ceiling, wondering what was going on. Kay was right in the middle of the bank and thought, "What do I do? If I leave it's going to look very odd, but if I stay it is going to get worse!" She stayed. The noise built up and up. Eventually bits of polystyrene started to fall from the ceiling. At that moment, fearing the ceiling would cave in, she rushed up to tell us that we could indeed be heard in the bank!

Since, through Jesus, the barrier has been removed, God hears us when we pray. We have immediate access to His presence, by the Spirit. We don't need to jump up and down to get His attention!

The Spirit helps us to pray. Not only does the Spirit bring us into the presence of God, He also helps us to pray (Romans 8:26). What matters is not the place in which we pray, the position we pray in or whether or not we use set forms of prayer; what matters is whether or not we are praying in the Spirit. All prayer should be led by the Spirit. Without His help prayer can easily become lifeless and dull. In the Spirit we are caught up in the Godhead, and prayer becomes the most important activity of our lives.

The Spirit helps us understand God's Word. Another part of developing our relationship with God is understanding what He is saying to us. Again the Spirit of God enables us to do this. Paul says, "I keep asking that the God of our Lord Jesus Christ, the glorious Father, may give you the Spirit of wisdom and revelation, so that you may know him better. I pray also that the eyes of your heart may be enlightened" (Ephesians 1:17, 18). The Spirit of God is a Spirit of wisdom and revelation. He enlightens our eyes so that, for example, we can understand what God is saying through the Bible.

Before I became a Christian I read and heard the Bible endlessly, but I did not understand it. It meant nothing to me. It did not make sense to me because I did not have the Spirit of God to interpret it. The Spirit of God is the best interpreter of what God has said.

Ultimately we will never understand Christianity without the Holy Spirit enlightening our eyes. We can see enough to make a step of faith, which is not a blind leap of faith; but real understanding often only follows faith. Anselm of Canterbury said, "I believe in order that I might understand."[37] Only when we believe and receive the Holy Spirit can we really understand God's revelation.

The Spirit of God helps us to develop our relationship with God, and He enables us to sustain that relationship. People are often worried that they will not be able to keep going in the Christian life. They are right to worry. We can't keep going by ourselves, but God by His Spirit keeps us going. It is the Spirit who brings us into a relationship with God and it is the Spirit who maintains that relationship. We are utterly dependent on Him.

THE FAMILY LIKENESS

I always find it fascinating to observe how children can look like both parents at the same time when the parents themselves may look so different. Even husbands and wives sometimes grow to look like each other as they spend time together over the years!

As we spend time in the presence of God, the Spirit of God transforms us. As Paul writes, "And we, who with unveiled faces all reflect the Lord's glory, are being transformed into his likeness with everincreasing glory, which comes from the Lord, who is the Spirit" (2 Corinthians 3:18). We are transformed into the moral likeness of Jesus Christ.

The fruit of the Spirit is developed in our lives. Paul tells us that "the fruit of the Spirit is love, joy, peace, patience, kindness, goodness, faithfulness, gentleness and self-control" (Galatians 5:22). These are the characteristics that the Spirit of God develops in our

141

lives. It is not that we become perfect immediately, but over a period of time there should be a change.

Love. The first and most important fruit of the Spirit is love. Love lies at the heart of the Christian faith. The Bible is the story of God's love for us. His desire is that we should respond by loving Him and loving our neighbor. The evidence of the work of the Spirit in our lives will be an increasing love for God and an increasing love for others. Without this love everything else counts for nothing.

Joy. Second in Paul's list is joy. Malcolm Muggeridge wrote: "The most characteristic and uplifting of the manifestations of conversion is rapture—an inexpressible joy which suffuses our whole being, making our fears dissolve into nothing, and our expectations all move heavenwards."[38] This joy is not dependent on our outward circumstances; it comes from the Spirit within. Richard Wurmbrand, who was imprisoned for many years and frequently tortured on account of his faith, wrote of this joy: "Alone in my cell, cold, hungry and in rags, I danced for joy every night … sometimes I was so filled with joy that I felt I would burst if I did not give it expression."[39]

Peace. The third fruit listed is peace. Detached from Christ, inner peace is a kind of spiritual marshmallow full of softness and sweetness but without much actual substance. The Greek word and Hebrew equivalent *shalom* means "wholeness," "soundness," "well-being," and "oneness with God." Every human heart longs for peace like that. Epictetus, the first-century pagan thinker, said, "While the Emperor may give peace from war on land and sea, he is unable to give peace from passion, grief and envy. He cannot give peace of heart, for which man yearns more than ever for outward peace."

It is wonderful to see those whose characters have been transformed into the likeness of Jesus Christ as these and the other fruit of the Spirit have grown in their lives. A woman in her eighties in our congregation said of a former pastor, "He gets more and more like our Lord." I cannot think of a higher compliment than that. It is the work of the Spirit of God to make us more and more like Jesus so that we carry the fragrance of the knowledge of him wherever we go (2 Corinthians 2:14).

UNITY IN THE FAMILY

When we come to Christ and become sons and daughters of God, we become part of a huge family. God's desire, like that of every normal parent, is that there should be unity in His family. Jesus prayed for unity among His followers (John 17). Paul pleaded with the Ephesian Christians to "make every effort to keep *the unity of the Spirit* through the bond of peace" (Ephesians 4:3, italics mine).

The same Holy Spirit lives in all Christians wherever they are, whatever their denomination, background, color, or race. The same Spirit is in every child of God, and His desire is that we should be united. Indeed, it is nonsense for the church to be divided because there is "*one* body and *one* Spirit ... *one* hope ... *one* Lord, *one* faith, *one* baptism; *one* God and Father of *all*, who is over *all* and through *all* and in *all*" (Ephesians 4:4-6, italics mine).

The same Spirit indwells Christians in Russia, China, Africa, the United States, England, or wherever. In one sense it is not so important what denomination we are—Roman Catholic, Lutheran, Methodist, Baptist, Pentecostal, Episcopalian, or independent. What is more important is whether or not we have the Spirit of God. If people have the Spirit of God living within them, they are Christians, and our brothers and sisters. It is a tremendous privilege to be part of this huge family; one of the great joys of coming to Christ is to experience this unity. There is a closeness and depth of relationship in the Christian church that I have never found outside of it. We must make every effort to keep the unity of the Spirit at every level: in our small groups, congregations, local church, and the worldwide church.

GIFTS FOR ALL THE CHILDREN

Although there is often a family likeness and, hopefully, unity in the family, there is also great variety. No two children are identical—not even identical twins are exactly alike. So it is in the body of Christ.

Every Christian is different; each has a different contribution to make, each has a different gift. The New Testament gives several lists of some of the gifts of the Spirit. In 1 Corinthians Paul lists nine gifts:

> Now to each one the manifestation of the Spirit is given for the common good. To one there is given through the Spirit the message of wisdom, to another the message of knowledge by means of the same Spirit, to another faith by the same Spirit, to another gifts of healing by that one Spirit, to another miraculous powers, to another prophecy, to another distinguishing between spirits, to another speaking in different kinds of tongues, and to still another the interpretation of tongues. All these are the work of one and the same Spirit, and he gives them to each one, just as he determines (1 Corinthians 12:7-11).

Elsewhere Paul mentions other gifts: apostles, teachers, helpers, administrators (1 Corinthians 12:28-30), evangelists and pastors (Ephesians 4), serving, encouraging, giving, leadership, showing mercy (Romans 12:7), hospitality, and speaking (1 Peter 4). No doubt these lists were not intended to be exhaustive.

All good gifts are from God, even if some, such as miracles, more obviously demonstrate the unusual acts of God in His world. Spiritual gifts include natural talents that have been transformed by the Holy Spirit. As the German theologian Jurgen Moltmann points out, "In principle every human potentiality and capacity can become

144

charismatic [that is, a gift of the Spirit] through a person's call, if only they are used in Christ."

These gifts are given to all Christians. The expression "to each one" runs like a thread through 1 Corinthians 12. Every Christian is part of the body of Christ. There are many different parts, but one body (vs. 12). We are baptized by (or in) one Spirit (vs. 13). We are all given the one Spirit to drink (vs. 13). There are no first- and second-class Christians. All Christians receive the Spirit. All Christians have spiritual gifts.

There is an urgent need for the gifts to be exercised. One of the major problems in the church at large is that so few are exercising their gifts. The church growth expert Eddie Gibbs said, "The present high level of unemployment in the nation pales into insignificance in comparison with that which prevails in the church."[40] As a result, a few people are left doing everything and are totally exhausted, while the rest are underutilized. The church has been likened to a soccer match, in which thousands of people desperately in need of exercise watch twenty-two people desperately in need of a rest!

The church cannot operate in maximum effectiveness until each person is playing his or her part. As David Watson, the writer and church leader, pointed out, "In different traditions, the church for years has been either pulpit-centred or altar-centred. In both situations the dominant role has been played by the minister or priest."[41] The church will only operate with maximum effectiveness when every person is using his or her gifts.

The Spirit of God gives each of us gifts. God does not require us to have many gifts, but He does require us to use what we have and to desire more (1 Corinthians 12:31; 14:1).

THE GROWING FAMILY

It is natural for families to grow. God said to Adam and Eve, "Be fruitful and multiply." It should be natural for the family of God to grow. Again, this is the work of the Spirit. Jesus said, "You will receive power when the Holy Spirit comes on you; and you will be my witnesses in Jerusalem, and in all Judea and Samaria, and to the ends of the earth" (Acts 1:8).

The Spirit of God gives us both the desire and the ability to tell others. The playwright Murray Watts tells the story of a young man who was convinced of the truth of Christianity, but was paralyzed with fear at the very thought of having to admit to being a Christian. The idea of telling anyone about his new-found faith, with all the dangers of being dubbed a religious nutcase, appalled him.

For many weeks he tried to banish the thought of religion from his mind, but it was no use. It was as if he heard a whisper in his conscience, repeating over and over again, "Follow me."

At last he could stand it no longer and he went to a very old man, who had been a Christian for the best part of a century. He told him of his nightmare, this terrible burden of "witnessing to the light," and how it stopped him from becoming a Christian. The man sighed and shook his head. "This is a matter between you and Christ," he said. "Why bring all these other people into it?" The young man nodded slowly.

"Go home," said the old man. "Go into your bedroom alone. Forget the world. Forget your family, and make it a secret between you and God."

The young man felt a weight fall from him as the old man spoke. "You mean, I don't have to tell anyone?"

"No," said the old man.

"No one at all?"

"Not if you don't want to."

Never had anyone dared to give the young man this advice before.

"Are you sure?" asked the young man, beginning to tremble with anticipation. "Can this be right?"

"It is right for you," said the old man.

So the young man went home, knelt down in prayer and was converted to Christ. Immediately, he ran down the stairs and into the kitchen, where his wife, father, and three friends were sitting. "Do you realize," he said, breathless with excitement, "that it's possible to be a Christian without telling anyone?"[42]

When we experience the Spirit of God we want to tell others. As we do, the family grows. The Christian family should never be static. It should be continually growing and drawing in new people, who themselves receive the power of the Holy Spirit and go out and tell others about Jesus.

I have stressed throughout this chapter that every Christian is indwelt by the Holy Spirit. Paul says, "If anyone does not have the Spirit of Christ, he does not belong to Christ" (Romans 8:9). Yet not every Christian is filled with the Spirit. Paul writes to the Christians at

Ephesus and says, "Be filled with the Spirit" (Ephesians 5:18). In the next chapter we will look at how we can be filled with the Spirit.

We started off the previous chapter with Genesis 1:1, 2 (the first verses in the Bible), and I want to end this chapter by looking at Revelation 22:17 (one of the last verses in the Bible). The Spirit of God is active throughout the Bible from Genesis to Revelation.

"The Spirit and the bride say, 'Come!' And let him who hears say, 'Come!' Whoever is thirsty, let him come; and whoever wishes, let him take the free gift of the water of life" (Revelation 22:17).

God wants to fill every one of us with His Spirit. Some people are longing for this. Some are not so sure that they want it—in which case they do not really have a thirst. If you do not have a thirst for more of the Spirit's fullness, why not pray for such a thirst? God takes us as we are. When we thirst and ask, God will give us "the free gift of the water of life."

10 How Can I Be Filled With the Spirit?

The evangelist J. John once addressed a conference on the subject of preaching. One of the points he made was that so often preachers exhort their hearers to do something, but they never tell them how to do it. They say, "Read your Bible." He wants to ask, "Yes, but how?" They say, "Pray more." He asks, "Yes, but how?" They say, "Tell people about Jesus." He asks, "Yes, but how?" In this chapter I want to look at the question of how we can be filled with the Spirit.[43]

We have an old gas boiler in our house. The pilot light is on all the time. But the boiler is not always giving out heat and power. Some have only got the pilot light of the Holy Spirit in their lives, whereas when people are filled with the Holy Spirit, they begin to fire on all cylinders (if you will forgive my mixing metaphors!). When you look at these people, you can almost see and feel the difference.

The Book of Acts has been described as Volume I of the history of the church. In it we see several examples of people experiencing the Holy Spirit. In an ideal world, every Christian would be filled with the Holy Spirit from the moment of conversion. Sometimes it happens like that (both in the New Testament and now), but not always—even in the New Testament. We have already looked at the first occasion of the outpouring of the Holy Spirit at Pentecost in Acts 2. As we go through Acts, we will see other examples.

When Peter and John prayed for the Samaritan believers and the Holy Spirit came upon them, Simon the Magician was so impressed he offered money in order to be able to do the same thing (Acts 8:14-18). Peter warned him that it was a terrible thing to try and buy God's gift with money. But the account shows that something very wonderful must have happened.

In the next chapter (Acts 9) we see one of the most remarkable conversions of all times. When Stephen, the first Christian martyr, was stoned, Saul approved his death (Acts 8:1) and afterwards began to destroy the church. Going from house to house, he dragged men and women off to prison (vs. 3). At the beginning of chapter 9 we find him still "breathing out murderous threats against the Lord's disciples (vs. 1)."

Within the space of a few days, Saul was preaching in synagogues that "Jesus is the Son of God" (vs. 20). He caused total astonishment, with people asking, "Isn't he the man who caused havoc in Jerusalem among those who call on this name [of Jesus] (vs. 21)?"

What had happened in those few days to change Saul so completely? First, he had encountered Jesus on the road to Damascus. Secondly, he had been filled with the Spirit (Acts 9:17). At that moment, "something like scales fell from Saul's eyes, and he could see again" (vs. 18). It sometimes happens that people who were not Christians, or who were even strongly anti-Christian, have a complete turnaround in their lives when they come to Christ and are filled with the Spirit. They can become powerful advocates of the Christian faith.

At Ephesus, Paul (as Saul was now called) came across a group who believed, but who had not even heard of the Holy Spirit. He placed his hands on them, the Holy Spirit came on them and they spoke in tongues and prophesied (Acts 19:1-7). There are people today who are in a similar position. They may have "believed" for some time or even all their lives. They may have been baptized, confirmed and gone to church from time to time or even regularly. Yet they may know little or nothing about the Holy Spirit.

I want to look at another incident early in the Book of Acts in a little more detail. It is the first occasion when Gentiles were filled with the Spirit. God did something extraordinary, which started with a vision given to a man called Cornelius. God also spoke to Peter through a vision and told him he wanted

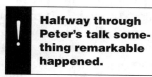

Halfway through Peter's talk something remarkable happened.

Peter to go and speak to the Gentiles at the house of this man Cornelius. Halfway through Peter's talk something remarkable happened: "The Holy Spirit came on all who heard the message. The circumcised believers [that is, the Jews] who had come with Peter were astonished that the gift of the Holy Spirit had been poured out even on the Gentiles. For they heard them speaking in tongues and praising God" (Acts 10:44-46). In the rest of this chapter I want to examine three aspects of what happened.

THEY EXPERIENCED THE POWER OF THE HOLY SPIRIT

Peter had to stop his talk because it was obvious that something was happening. The filling of the Spirit rarely happens imperceptibly, although the experience is different for everyone.

In the description of the Day of Pentecost (Acts 2), Luke uses the language of a heavy tropical rainstorm. It is a picture of the power of the Spirit flooding the apostles' beings. There were physical manifestations. They heard a gale (vs. 2); it was not a real gale, but it resembled one. It was the mighty invisible power of the *ruach* of God; this is the same word, as we have seen, for wind, breath, and spirit in the Old Testament. Sometimes, when people are filled, they shake like a leaf in the wind. Others find themselves breathing deeply as if almost physically breathing in the Spirit.

They also saw something that resembled fire (Acts 2:3). Physical heat sometimes accompanies the filling of the Spirit and people experience it in their hands or some other part of their bodies. One person described a feeling of glowing all over. Another said she experienced "liquid heat." Still another described "burning in my arms when I was not hot." Fire perhaps symbolizes the power, passion, and purity the Spirit of God brings to our lives.

For others, the experience of the Spirit may be an overwhelming experience of the love of God. Paul prays for the Christians at Ephesus that they might have "power, together with all the saints, to grasp how wide and long and high and deep is the love of Christ" (Ephesians 3:18). The love of Christ is wide enough to reach every person in the world. It reaches across every continent to people of every race, color, tribe, and background. It is long enough to last throughout a lifetime and into eternity. It is deep enough to reach us however far we have fallen. It is high enough to lift us into the heavenly places. We see this love supremely in the cross of Christ. We know Christ's love for us because He was willing to die for us. Paul prayed that we would grasp the

Fire symbolizes the power, passion, and purity the Spirit brings to our lives.

extent of this love.

Yet he does not stop there. He goes on to pray that we would "know this love that surpasses knowledge—that you may be filled to the measure of all the fullness of God" (Ephesians 3:19). It is not enough to understand His love; we need to experience His love that surpasses knowledge. It is often as people are filled with the Spirit— "filled to the measure of all the fullness of God" (vs. 19)—that they experience in their hearts this transforming love of Christ.

Thomas Goodwin, one of the Puritans of three hundred years ago, illustrated this experience. He pictured a man walking along a road hand in hand with his little boy. The little boy knows that this man is his father, and that his father loves him. But suddenly the father stops, picks up the boy, lifts him into his arms, embraces him, kisses him, and hugs him. Then he puts him down again and they continue walking. It is a wonderful thing to be walking along holding your father's hand; but it is an incomparably greater thing to have his arms enfolded around you.

"He has embraced us," says Spurgeon, and He pours His love upon us and He "hugs" us. Martyn Lloyd-Jones quotes these examples among many others in his book on Romans, and comments on the experience of the Spirit:

> Let us realize then the profound character of the experience. This is not light and superficial and ordinary; it is not something of which you can say, "Don't worry about your feelings." Worry about your feelings? You will have such a depth of feeling that for a moment you may well imagine that you have never "felt" anything in your life before. It is the profoundest experience that a man can ever know.[43]

THEY WERE RELEASED IN PRAISE

When these Gentiles were filled with the Spirit they started "praising

153

God." Spontaneous praise is the language of people who are excited and thrilled about their experience of God. It should involve our whole personality, including our emotions. I am asked, "Is it right to express emotions in church? Isn't there a danger of emotionalism?"

The danger for most of us in our relationship with God is not emotionalism, but a lack of emotion—a lack of feeling. Our relationship with God can be rather cold. Every relationship of love involves our emotions. Of course, there must be more than emotions. There must be friendship, communication, understanding, and service. But if I never showed any emotion towards my wife, my love for her would lack something. If we do not experience any emotion in our relationship with God, then our whole personality is not involved. We are called to love, praise, and worship God with all of our beings.

Every relationship of love involves our emotions.

It could be argued that emotions are all right in private, but what about the public demonstration of emotion? After a conference at Brighton attended by the Archbishop of Canterbury, *The Times* carried correspondence about the place of emotions in church. Under the title "Carey's Charisms" one man wrote:

> Why is it that if a cinema comedy produces laughter, the film is regarded as successful; if a theatre tragedy brings tears to the audience the production is regarded as touching; if a football match thrills the spectators, the game is reviewed as exciting; but if the congregation are moved by the glory of God in worship, the audience are accused of emotionalism?

Of course, there is such a thing as emotionalism where emotions take precedence over the solid foundation of teaching from the Bible. But as the former Bishop of Coventry, Cuthbert Bardsley, once said, "The chief danger of the Anglican church is not delirious emotionalism." One might add, "Nor in many other churches." Our worship of God should involve our whole personality, mind, heart, will, and emotions.

THEY RECEIVED A NEW LANGUAGE

As on the Day of Pentecost and with the Ephesian Christians (Acts 19), when the Gentiles were filled with the Spirit they received the gift of tongues. The word for "tongues" is the same word as that for "languages," and it means the ability to speak in a language you have never learned. It may be an angelic language (1 Corinthians 13:1), which presumably is not recognizable, or it may be a recognizable human language (as at Pentecost). A young woman called Penny in our congregation was praying with another woman. She ran out of words in English and started praying in tongues. Her friend smiled and then opened her eyes and started laughing. She said, "You have just spoken to me in Russian." The friend, although English, spoke fluent Russian and had a great love for the language. Penny asked, "What have I been saying?" The friend told Penny that she had been saying, "My dear child," over and over again. Penny does not speak a single word of Russian. For that young woman those three words were of great significance. She was assured that she was important to God.

The gift of tongues has brought great blessing to many people. It is, as we have seen, one of the gifts of the Spirit. It is not the only gift or even the most important gift. Not all Christians speak in tongues, nor is it necessarily a sign of being filled with the Spirit. It is possible to be filled with the Spirit and not speak in tongues. Nevertheless, for many, both in the New Testament and in Christian experience, speaking in tongues accompanies an experience of the Holy Spirit and may be the first experience of the more obviously supernatural activity of the Spirit. Many today are puzzled by the gift. Hence, I have devoted quite a lot of space in this chapter to the subject. In 1 Corinthians 14 Paul deals with a number of questions often raised.

What exactly is speaking in tongues?

Speaking in tongues is a form of prayer (one of the many different forms of prayer found in the New Testament), according to Paul, "for anyone who speaks in a tongue does not speak to men but to *God*" (1 Corinthians 14:2, italics mine). It is a form of prayer that builds up the individual Christian (vs. 4). Obviously, the gifts that directly edify the church are even more important, but this does not make tongues unimportant. The benefit of tongues is that it is a form of prayer that transcends the limitation of human language. This seems to be what Paul means when he says "For if I pray in a tongue, my spirit prays, but my mind is unfruitful" (1 Corinthians 14:14).

Tongues is prayer that transcends the limitation of human language.

Everybody is limited by language. I am told the average Englishman knows five thousand English words. Winston Churchill apparently used fifteen thousand words. But even he was limited to that extent. Often people are frustrated that they cannot express what they really feel, even in a human relationship. They feel things in their spirits, but they do not know how to put their feelings into words. This is often true also in our relationship with God.

This is where the gift of tongues can be a great help. It enables us to express to God what we really feel in our spirits without going through the process of translating it into English. (Hence Paul says, "My mind is unfruitful.") It is not mindless; it is unfruitful because it is not going through the process of translation into an intelligible language.

In what areas does speaking in tongues help?

Many people have found this gift especially helpful in three areas.

Praise and worship. We are particularly limited in our language. When children (or even adults) write thank-you letters it is not long before they run out of language, and we find that words such as "lovely," "wonderful," or "brilliant" are repeated over and over again. In our praise and worship of God we can often find language limiting.

We long to express our love, worship and praise of God, particularly when we are filled with the Spirit. The gift of tongues enables us to do this without the limitation of human language.

Prayer under pressure. Speaking in tongues can be a great help when praying under pressure. There are times in our lives when it is hard to know exactly how to pray. It can be because we are burdened by many pressures, anxieties, or griefs. Not long ago I prayed for a man aged twenty-six whose wife had died of cancer after only one year of married life. He asked for and instantly received the gift of tongues; all the things that he had pushed down in his life seemed to pour out. He told me afterwards what a relief it had been to be able to unburden all those things.

I, too, have found this in my own experience. In 1987 during a staff meeting at our church, I received a message saying that my mother had had a heart attack and was in the hospital. As I dashed up to the main road and caught a taxi to the hospital, I had never been more grateful for the gift of tongues. I desperately wanted to pray, but felt too shocked to form any sentences in English. The gift of tongues enabled me to pray all the way to the hospital and to bring the situation to God in a time of crisis.

Prayer for others. Many people have found the gift a help in praying for other people. It is hard to pray for others, especially if you have not seen them or heard from them for some time. After a while, "Lord, bless them" might be our most elaborate prayer. It can be a real help to start praying in tongues for them. Often, as we do that, God gives us the words to pray in English.

It is not selfish to want to pray in tongues. Although, "he who speaks in a tongue edifies himself" (1 Corinthians 14:4), the indirect effects of this can be very great. Jackie Pullinger describes the transformation in her ministry when she began to use the gift:

> By the clock I prayed 15 minutes a day in the language of the Spirit and still felt nothing as I asked the Spirit to help me intercede for those he wanted to reach. After about six weeks of this I began to lead people to Jesus without trying. Gangsters fell to their knees sobbing in the streets, women were healed, heroin addicts were miraculously set free. And I knew it all had nothing to do with me.

It was also the gateway for her to receive other gifts of the Spirit:

> With my friends I began to learn about the other gifts of the Spirit and we experienced a remarkable few years of ministry. Scores of gangsters and well-to-do people, students and churchmen, were converted and all received a new language to pray in private and other gifts to use when meeting together. We opened several homes to house heroin addicts and all were delivered from drugs painlessly because of the power of the Holy Spirit.[45]

Does Paul approve of speaking in tongues?

The context of 1 Corinthians 14 is excessive public use in church of the gift of tongues. Paul says, "*In the church* I would rather speak five intelligible words to instruct others than ten thousand words in a tongue" (vs. 19, italics mine). There would be little point in Paul arriving at Corinth and giving his sermon in tongues. They would not be able to understand unless there was someone to interpret. So he lays down guidelines for the public use of tongues (vs. 27).

Nevertheless, Paul makes it clear that speaking in tongues should not be forbidden (vs. 39). With regard to the private use of this gift (on our own with God), he strongly encourages it. He says, "I would like every one of you to speak in tongues" (vs. 5) and, "I thank God that I speak in tongues more than all of you" (vs. 18). This does not mean that every Christian has to speak in tongues or that we are second-class Christians if we do not speak in tongues. There is no such thing as first- and second-class Christians. Nor does it mean that God loves us any less if we don't yet speak in tongues. Nevertheless, the gift of tongues is a blessing from God.

How do we receive the gift of tongues?

Some say, "I don't want the gift of tongues." God will never force you to receive a gift. Tongues is just one of the wonderful gifts of the Spirit, and not the only one by any means, as we saw in the last chapter. Like every gift it has to be received by faith.

Not every Christian speaks in tongues. Yet Paul says, "I would like every one of you to speak in tongues," suggesting that it is not only for a special class of Christians. It is open to all Christians. There is no reason why anyone who wants this gift should not receive it. Paul is not saying that speaking in tongues is the be-all and end-all of the Christian life; he is saying that it is a very helpful gift. If you would like to receive it, there is no reason why you should not.

Like all the gifts of God, we have to cooperate with His Spirit. God does not force His gifts on us. When I first became a Christian I read somewhere that the gifts of the Spirit went out in the apostolic age (that is, the first century). Tongues were not for today. When I heard about speaking in tongues I decided to confirm that they were not for today, so I prayed for the gift—and then kept my mouth firmly shut! I didn't start praying in tongues and felt that this proved that the gifts had gone out with the apostles.

One day two friends of mine, who had just been filled with the Spirit and received the gift of tongues, came to see me. I told them quite firmly that the gifts of the Spirit had gone out with the apostolic age, but I could see the difference it had made to them. There was a new radiance about them, and there still is years later. I decided to ask the people who had prayed for them to pray for me to be filled with the Spirit and to receive the gift of tongues. As they did, I experienced the power of the Holy Spirit. They explained to me that if I wanted to receive the gift of tongues I had to cooperate with the Spirit of God; I needed to open my mouth and start to speak to God in any language but English or another known to me. As I did, I received the gift of tongues also.

WHAT ARE COMMON HINDRANCES TO BEING FILLED WITH THE SPIRIT?

On one occasion Jesus was speaking to His disciples on the subject of prayer and the Holy Spirit (Luke 11:9-13). In that passage He deals with some of the principal difficulties we may have in receiving gifts from God.

Doubt

People have many doubts in this whole area, the principal one being, "If I ask will I receive?"

Jesus says simply: "I say to you: Ask and it will be given to you."

Jesus must have seen that they were a little skeptical because He repeats it in a different way: "Seek and you will find."

And again He says a third time: "Knock and the door will be opened to you."

He knows human nature, so He goes on a fourth time: "For everyone who asks receives."

160

They are not convinced, so He says it a fifth time: "He who seeks finds."

Again, a sixth time: "To him who knocks, the door will be opened."

Why does He say it six times? Because He knows what we are like. We find it very difficult to believe that God would give us anything— let alone something as unusual and wonderful as His Holy Spirit and the gifts that come with the Spirit.

Fear

Even if we have cleared the first hurdle of doubt, some of us trip up on the next hurdle of fear. The fear is about what we will receive. Will it be something good?

Jesus uses the analogy of a human father. If a child asks for a fish, no father would give him a snake. If a child asks for an egg, no father would give him a scorpion (Luke 11:11, 12). It is unthinkable that we would treat our children like that. Jesus goes on to say that, in comparison with God, we are evil! If we would not treat our children like that, it is inconceivable that God would treat us like that. He is not going to let us down. If we ask for the Holy Spirit and all the wonderful gifts he brings, that is exactly what we will receive (Luke 11:13).

Inadequacy

Of course, it is important that there is no unforgiveness or other sin in our lives, and that we have turned our back on all that we know is wrong. However, even after we have done that, we often have a vague feeling of unworthiness and inadequacy. We cannot believe that God would give *us* anything. We can believe that He would give gifts to very advanced Christians, but not to us. But Jesus does not say, "How much more will your Father in heaven give the Holy Spirit to all very advanced Christians." He says, "How much more will your Father in heaven give the Holy Spirit to *those who ask him*" (Luke 11:13, italics mine).

If you would like to be filled with the Spirit, you might like to find someone who would pray for you. If you don't have anyone who would be able to pray for you, nothing stops you from praying on your own. Some are filled with the Spirit without receiving the gift of tongues. The two do not necessarily go together. Yet in the New Testament and in experience they often do go together. There is no reason why we should not pray for both.

If you are praying on your own:

1. Ask God to forgive you for anything that could be a barrier to receiving.

2. Turn from any area of your life that you know is wrong.

3. Ask God to fill you with His Spirit. Go on seeking Him until you find. Go on knocking until the door opens. Seek God with all your heart.

4. If you would like to receive the gift of tongues, ask. Then open your mouth and start to praise God in any language but English or any other language known to you.

5. Believe that what you receive is from God. Don't let anyone tell you that you made it up. (It is most unlikely that you have.)

6. Persevere. Languages take time to develop. Most of us start with a very limited vocabulary. Gradually it develops. Tongues is like that. It takes time to develop the gift. But don't give up.

7. If you have prayed for any other gift, seek opportunities to use it. Remember that all gifts have to be developed by use.

Being filled with the Spirit is not a one-time experience. Peter was filled with the Spirit three times in the space of chapters 2–4 in the Book of Acts (Acts 2:4; 4:8, 31). When Paul says, "Be filled with the Spirit" (Ephesians 5:18), he uses the present continuous tense, urging them and us to go on and on being filled with the Spirit.

11 | How Can I Resist Evil?

There is a close connection between good and God and between evil and the devil. Indeed, in the English language, the difference is only one letter! Behind the power of good lies Goodness Himself. Directly or indirectly behind our own evil desires and the temptations of the world lies evil personified—the devil.

Because there is so much evil in the world, some find it easier to believe in the devil than in God. "As far as God goes, I am a nonbeliever ... but when it comes to the devil—well, that's something else ... the devil keeps advertising. ... the devil does lots of commercials," said William Peter Blatty who wrote and produced *The Exorcist.*[46]

On the other hand, many Westerners find belief in the devil more difficult than belief in God. This may be partly because of a false image of what the devil is like. If the image of God as a white-bearded old man sitting on a cloud is absurd and incredible, so also is the image of a horned devil trudging through Dante's inferno. We are not dealing with an alien from outer space but with a real personal force of evil who is active in the world today.

Once we have come to believe in a transcendent God, in some ways it is only logical to accept belief in a devil. Michael Green said:

> Belief in a great transcendent power of evil adds nothing whatever to the difficulties imposed by belief in a transcendent power of good. Indeed, it eases them somewhat. For if there were no Satan, it would be hard to resist the conclusion that God is a fiend both

because of what he does, in nature, and what he allows, in human wickedness.[47]

According to the biblical worldview, behind the evil in the world lies the devil. The Greek word for the devil, *diabolos*, translates the Hebrew word *satan*. We are not told very much about the origins of Satan in the Bible. There is a hint that he may have been a fallen angel (Isaiah 14:12-23). He appears on a few occasions in the books of the Old Testament (Job 1; 1 Chronicles 21:1). He is not merely a force but is personal.

We are given a clearer picture of his activities in the New Testament. The devil is a personal spiritual being who is in active rebellion against God and has the leadership of many demons like himself. Paul tells us to take our "stand against the devil's schemes. For our struggle is not against flesh and blood, but against the rulers, against the authorities … against the spiritual forces of evil in the heavenly realms" (Ephesians 6:11, 12).

The devil and his angels, according to Paul, are not to be underestimated. They are cunning ("the devil's schemes," vs. 11). They are powerful ("rulers," "authorities," and "forces," vs. 12). They are evil ("forces of evil," vs. 12). Therefore, we should not be surprised when we come under a powerful assault from the enemy.

Why should we believe in the devil?

Why should we believe in the existence of the devil? Some say, "Nowadays you can't believe in the devil." However, there are very good reasons to believe in his existence.

First, belief in Satan's existence is biblical. That is not to say that the Bible concentrates on the devil. Satan is not mentioned very often in the Old Testament, and it is only when we come to the New Testament that the doctrine is developed more fully. Jesus clearly believed in the existence of Satan and was tempted by him. Jesus frequently cast out demons, freeing people from the forces of evil and sin in their lives, and gave His disciples authority to do the same. The rest of the New Testament contains many references to the work of the devil (1 Peter 5:8-11; Ephesians 6:1-12).

Secondly, Christians down the ages have almost invariably believed in the existence of the devil. The early church theologians, the reformers, the great evangelists like Wesley and Whitefield, and the overwhelming majority of men and women of God, knew that there were very real spiritual forces of evil around. As soon as we start to serve the Lord, the devil's interest is aroused. According to Jean-Baptiste Vianney, "The devil only tempts those souls that wish to abandon sin … the others belong to him: he has no need to tempt them."[48]

Thirdly, common sense confirms the existence of the devil. Any kind of theology that ignores the existence of a personal devil has a great deal to explain: evil regimes, institutional torture and violence, mass murders, brutal rapes, large-scale drug trafficking, terrorist atrocities, sexual and physical abuse of children, occult activity, and satanic rituals. Who is behind all this? A ditty goes like this:

Some say the devil's been,
Some say the devil's gone,
But simple people, like you and me,
Would like to know, who carries the business on?

Scripture, tradition, and reason all point to the existence of the devil. This does not mean that we should become obsessed by him. As C. S. Lewis points out, "There are two equal and opposite errors into which our race can fall about the devils [demons]. One is to disbelieve in their existence. The other is to believe, and to feel an excessive and unhealthy interest in them. They themselves are equally pleased by both errors and hail a materialist or a magician with the same delight."[49]

Concerning a disbelief in Satan, Michael Green has said:

Like any general who can persuade the opposition to underestimate him, Satan ... must be enchanted at the present state of affairs which leaves him free to operate with the maximum of ease and efficiency, confident that nobody takes him seriously. The more he can do to encourage this doubt of his existence, the better. The more he can blind people's minds to the true state of affairs, the better his aims are furthered.[48]

Many fall into the opposite danger of having an excessive and unhealthy interest in him. There is a whole new interest in spiritualism, palm-reading, ouija boards, channeling (consulting the dead), astrology, horoscopes, witchcraft, and occult powers. Involvement in these things is expressly forbidden in Scripture (Deuteronomy 18:10; Leviticus 19:26 and following; Galatians 5:19 and following; Revelation 21:8; 22:15). If we have meddled in any of these things, we can be forgiven. We need to repent and destroy anything associated with that activity such as books, charms, videos, and magazines (Acts 19:19).

Christians, too, can have an unhealthy interest in these things. A new Christian recently showed me a couple of supposedly Christian books where the whole emphasis was on the work of the enemy—with a lot of space devoted to speculation concerning the number of the beast in Revelation, and tying this in with credit cards! The intention was good, I am sure, but the focus on the work of the enemy seemed to me to be unhealthy. The Bible never has this kind of focus. The spotlight is always on God.

WHAT ARE THE DEVIL'S TACTICS?

The ultimate aim of Satan is to destroy every human being (John 10:10). He wants us to follow a path that leads to destruction. To that end, he tries to prevent anyone coming to faith in Jesus Christ. Paul

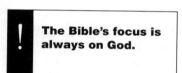

The Bible's focus is always on God.

tells us: "The god of this age [the devil] has blinded the minds of unbelievers, so that they cannot see the light of the gospel of the glory of Christ, who is the image of God" (2 Corinthians 4:4).

So long as we are going along Satan's path and our eyes are blinded, we will probably be almost totally unaware of his tactics. Once we start walking along the path that leads to life and our eyes are opened to the truth, we become aware that we are under attack.

The initial line of attack is often in the area of doubt. We see this in the opening chapters of Genesis where the enemy, in the form of a serpent, says to Eve, "Did God really say ...?" His opening move is to raise a doubt in her mind.

We see the same tactic in the temptation of Jesus. The devil comes to him and says, "*If* you are the Son of God ... " (Matthew 4:3, italics mine). First, he raises doubts, then come the temptations. His tactics have not changed. He still raises doubts in our mind: "Did God really say that such and such a course of action is wrong?" or, "If you are a Christian ..." He tries to undermine our confidence in what God has said and in our relationship with Him. We need to recognize this source of many of our doubts.

Raising doubts was the precursor to the main attack on both Eve in the Garden of Eden and Jesus in the wilderness. In Genesis 3, we see an exposé of the way in which Satan, who is described as "the tempter" (Matthew 4:2), so often works.

Permission and penalty. In Genesis 2:16, 17, God gave Adam and Eve a far-reaching permission ("You are free to eat from any tree in the garden"), one prohibition ("But you must not eat from the tree of the knowledge of good and evil"), and then warned them of the penalty if they disobeyed ("For when you eat of it you will surely die").

Satan ignores the wide scope of the permission and concentrates on the one prohibition—which he then exaggerates (Genesis 3:1). His tactics have not changed. He still ignores the permission. He ignores the fact that God has given us all things richly to enjoy (1 Timothy 6:17). He ignores the great blessing of walking in a relationship with God. He ignores the riches of Christian marriages and families, the security of a Christian home, the level of friendship that we can enjoy as Christians, and countless other things that God offers to those who know and love Him. He does not tell us about these things. Instead he concentrates on a tiny unimaginative list of prohibitions of what Christians are not allowed to do—reminding us again and again that we can't get drunk, swear, or be promiscuous. There are relatively few things that God does not allow us to do and there are very good reasons why He prohibits them.

Finally, the devil denies the penalty. He says, "You will not surely die" (Genesis 3:4). He says, in effect, that it will not do you any harm to disobey God. He suggests to us that God is really a spoilsport, that God does not want the best for our lives and that we will miss out if we don't disobey. In fact the opposite is the case, as Adam and Eve found out. It is disobedience that causes us to miss out on so much of what God intended for us.

Consequences of disobedience. In the verses that follow, we see the consequences of disobeying God. First, there is shame and embarrassment. Adam and Eve felt exposed and began a cover-up opera-

> **Deep down, we all feel ashamed and embarrassed by our sin.**

tion (Genesis 3:7). How quickly would we want to leave the room if every action we had ever done was displayed on a screen, followed by a written list of every thought we had ever entertained? Deep down, we all feel ashamed and embarrassed by our sin. We don't want people to find us out. Sir Arthur Conan Doyle once played a practical joke on twelve men. They were all very well-known, respected, and respectable men, regarded as pillars of the establishment. He sent each of them a telegram, with the same message in each: "Flee at once. All is discovered." Within twenty-four hours, they had all fled the country! Virtually all of us have something in our lives of which we are ashamed; something we would not want everyone to know about. We often put up barriers around us to avoid the possibility of being found out.

Broken relationship. Next, Adam and Eve's friendship with God was broken. When they heard God coming, they hid (Genesis 3:8). Many people today shy away from God. They don't want to face up to the fact of the possibility of His existence. Like Adam they are afraid (vs. 10). Some have a real fear of going to church or mixing with

171

Christians. A couple in our congregation told me about a 224-pound rugby player from Australia whom they had invited to church. He got as far as the drive, then he started shaking in the car. He said, "I can't go. I'm too frightened to go into the church." He could not look God in the face. There was a separation between him and God, just as there was with Adam and Eve. God immediately started to try and draw them back into a relationship. He called out, "Where are you?" (vs. 9). He still does.

Then, there is a separation between Adam and Eve themselves. Adam blames Eve. Eve blames the devil. But they and we are responsible for our own sin. We cannot blame God or others or even the devil (James 1:13-15). We see this in our society today. When people turn away from God, they start fighting one another. We see the breakdown of relationships wherever we look: broken marriages, broken homes, broken relationships at work, civil war, and war between nations.

Finally, we see in God's punishment of Adam and Eve (vss. 14 onwards) that they were deceived by Satan. We see how his deception led Adam and Eve away from God on to a path which, as Satan knew from the beginning, led to destruction.

We see that Satan is a deceiver, a destroyer, a tempter, and one who raises doubts. He is also an accuser. The Hebrew word for Satan means "accuser" or "slanderer." He accuses God before people. God gets the blame for everything. God, he says, is not to be trusted. Secondly, he accuses Christians before God (Revelation 12:10). He denies the power of the death of Jesus. He condemns us and makes us feel guilty—not for any particular sin, but with a general and vague feeling of guilt. In contrast, when the Holy Spirit draws attention to a sin, He identifies it so that we can turn from it.

> **! Satan wants failure to become a pattern in our lives.**

Temptation is not the same thing as sin. Sometimes the devil puts a thought into our mind that we know is wrong. At that moment we have a choice whether to accept it or reject it. If we accept it, we are on the way towards sin. If we reject it, we do what Jesus did. He was "tempted in every way, just as we are—yet was without sin" (Hebrews 4:15). When Satan put evil thoughts in His mind, He rejected them. But often before we have the chance to decide one way or the other, Satan accuses us. Within a split second he says, "Look at you! Call yourself a Christian? What was that you were thinking about? You can't be a Christian. What a terrible thing to think!" He wants us to agree and say, "Oh no! I can't be a Christian," or, "Oh no! I've blown it now, so it doesn't matter if I blow it a bit more!" We are on the way down, and this is his aim. The tactics are those of condemnation and accusation. If he can provoke guilt in us, he knows the thought is: "It doesn't really make any difference now if I do it or not. I have already failed." So we do it and temptation becomes sin.

Satan wants failure to become a pattern in our lives. He knows that the more we fall into sin, the more sin will start to control our lives. The first injection of heroin may not be enough to addict you, but if you inject it day after day, month after month, it gets a grip and you become an addict. It has taken hold of you. If we fall into a pattern of doing things that we know to be wrong, these things grip our lives. We become addicted and we are on the path that Satan desires—the one that leads to destruction (Matthew 7:13).

WHAT IS OUR POSITION?

As Christians, God has rescued us from "the dominion of darkness and brought us into the kingdom of the Son he loves" (Colossians 1:13). Before we were Christians, Paul says, we were in the dominion of darkness. Satan ruled us and we were subject to sin, slavery, death, and destruction. That is what the dominion of darkness is like.

Now, Paul says, we have been transferred from the kingdom of darkness to the kingdom of light. The moment we come to Christ we are transferred from darkness to light, and in the kingdom of light, Jesus is King. There is forgiveness, freedom, life, and salvation. Once we have been transferred, we belong to someone else: to Jesus Christ and His kingdom. Hockey great Wayne Gretzky played many years for the Los Angeles Kings. In 1996, he became a free agent and entertained offers from other teams. He accepted an offer from the St. Louis Blues. Suppose that the manager of the Kings should call Gretzky and say, "Why weren't you at the practice this morning?" Gretzky would reply, "I don't work for you any more. I have been transferred. I am working for another team" (or at least that is the gist of what he would say!).

Jesus has transferred us to a new kingdom.

In a far more wonderful way, we have been transferred from the kingdom of darkness where Satan is in charge, to the kingdom of God where Jesus is in charge. When Satan asks us to do his work our reply is, "I don't belong to you any more."

Satan is a conquered foe (Luke 10:17-20). On the cross Jesus "disarmed the powers and authorities" and "made a public spectacle of them, triumphing over them by the cross" (Colossians 2:15). Satan and all his minions were defeated at the cross, and that is why Satan and his demons are so frightened of the name of Jesus (Acts 16:18). They know they are defeated.

Jesus has freed us from guilt, so we don't need to be condemned. He has set us free from addictions. Jesus broke the power of these things and set us free. He broke the fear of death when he defeated death. With that, He set us free, potentially, from every fear. All these things—guilt, addiction, and fear—belong to the kingdom of darkness. Jesus has transferred us to a new kingdom.

The Cross was a great victory over Satan and his minions, and we now live in the time of the mopping-up operations. Although the enemy is not yet destroyed and is still capable of inflicting casualties, he is disarmed, defeated, and demoralized. This is our position, and it is vital to realize the strength of the position we are in, due to the victory of Jesus on the cross for us.

HOW DO WE DEFEND OURSELVES?

Since the war is not over and Satan is not yet destroyed, we need to make sure that our defenses are in order. Paul tells us to "put on the full armor of God so that you can take your stand against the devil's schemes" (Ephesians 6:11). He then mentions six pieces of equipment that we need. Sometimes it is said, "The secret of the Christian life is …" But there is no one secret; we need all the armor.

Belt of truth

First, we need the "belt of truth" (vs. 14). This probably means the foundation of Christian doctrine and truth. It means getting the whole Christian truth (or as much of it as one can) into our systems. We do this by reading the Bible, listening to sermons and talks, reading Christian books, and listening to tapes. This will enable us to distinguish what is true and what are Satan's lies, for Satan is "a liar and the father of lies" (John 8:44).

Breastplate of righteousness

Next, we need the "breastplate of righteousness" (vs. 14). This is the righteousness that comes from God through what Jesus has done on the cross. It enables us to be in a relationship with God and to live a righteous life. We need to resist the devil. The apostle James says, "Resist the devil, and he will flee from you. Come near to God and he will come near to you" (James 4:7, 8). We all fall from time to time.

175

When we do we need to get up quickly. We do this by telling God how sorry we are for what we have done, being as specific as possible (1 John 1:9). He then promises to restore His friendship with us.

Shoes of the gospel of peace

Then, we also need the "shoes of the gospel of peace" (Ephesians 6:15). I understand this to mean a readiness to speak about the Gospel of Jesus Christ. As John Wimber often says, "It is hard to sit still and be good." If we are constantly seeking opportunities to pass on the Good News, we have an effective defense against the enemy. Once we declare our Christian faith to our families and at work, we strengthen our defense. It is hard, because we know that we are being watched to see if we live up to our faith. But it is a great incentive to do so.

Shield of faith

The fourth piece of armor is the "shield of faith" (vs. 16). With this, we "can extinguish all the flaming arrows of the evil one." Faith is the opposite of cynicism and skepticism, which wreak havoc in many lives. One aspect of faith has been defined as "taking a promise of God and daring to believe it." Satan will throw his arrows of doubt to undermine us—but with the shield of faith we resist him.

Helmet of salvation

Fifth, Paul tells us to "take the helmet of salvation" (vs. 17). As Bishop Westcott, Regius Professor of Divinity at Cambridge, once pointed out, there are three tenses of salvation. We have been saved from the penalty of sin. We are being saved from the power of sin. We shall be saved from the presence of sin. We need to grasp these great concepts in our mind; to know them so that we can answer the enemy's doubts and accusations.

Sword of the Spirit

Finally, we are to take "the sword of the Spirit, which is the word of God" (vs. 17). Probably here Paul is thinking of the Scriptures. Jesus used the Scriptures when Satan attacked. Each time Jesus replied with the Word of God, and in the end Satan had to leave. It is well worthwhile to learn verses from the Bible, which we can use to ward off the enemy and remind ourselves of the promises of God.

HOW DO WE ATTACK?

As we have already seen, Satan and his minions were defeated on the cross, and we are now involved in the final mopping-up operations before the return of Jesus. As Christians, we need not be afraid of Satan; he has a great deal to fear from the activity of Christians.

Prayer

We are called to pray. We are involved in spiritual warfare, though "the weapons we fight with are not the weapons of the world. On the contrary, they have divine power to demolish strongholds" (2 Corinthians 10:4). Prayer was a very high priority for Jesus, and it should be for us. In the words of the hymn, "Satan trembles when he sees the weakest Christian on his knees."

Action

We are also called to action. In the life of Jesus, prayer and action went hand in hand. Jesus proclaimed the kingdom of God, healed the sick, and cast out demons. He commissioned His disciples to do the same. Later on we will look in more detail at what this means.

It is important to stress the greatness of God and the relative powerlessness of the enemy. We do not believe that there are two equal and opposite powers—God and Satan. That is not the biblical picture. God is the creator of the universe. Satan is a part of His creation—a fallen part. He is a small part. Further, he is a defeated enemy and is about to be utterly wiped out when Jesus returns (Revelation 12:12).

In a superb picture in C. S. Lewis' book, *The Great Divorce*, he speaks about hell as the place where Satan and his demons operate. A man has arrived in heaven and is being shown round by his "teacher." He goes down on hands and knees, takes a blade of grass and, using the thin end as a pointer, he eventually finds a tiny crack in the soil in which is concealed the whole of hell:

> "Do you mean then that Hell—all that infinite empty town—is down in some little crack like this?"
>
> "Yes. All Hell is smaller than one pebble of your earthly world: but it is smaller than one atom of this world, the Real World. Look at yon butterfly. If it swallowed all Hell, Hell would not be big enough to do it any harm or to have any taste."
>
> "It seems big enough when you are in it, Sir."
>
> "And yet all loneliness, angers, hatreds, envies and itchings that it contains, if rolled into one single experience and put into

the scale against the least moment of the joy that is felt by the least in Heaven, would have no weight that could be registered at all. Bad cannot succeed even in being bad as truly as good is good. If all Hell's miseries together entered the consciousness of yon wee yellow bird on the bough there, they would be swallowed up without trace, as if one drop of ink had been dropped into that Great Ocean to which your terrestrial Pacific itself is only a molecule."[50]

12 Why and How Should We Tell Others?

Why should we talk about our Christian faith? Isn't it a private matter? Isn't the best sort of Christian the one who just lives the Christian life? Sometimes people say to me, "I know someone who is a fine Christian. She has a strong faith—but she does not talk about it. Isn't that the highest form of Christianity?"

The short answer is that someone must have told that person about the Christian faith. The slightly longer answer is that there are good reasons for telling others about Jesus. First, it is a command of Jesus Himself. Tom Forrest, the Roman Catholic priest who first suggested to the Pope the idea of calling the 1990s "The Decade of Evangelism," points out that the word "go" appears 1,514 times in the Bible (*Revised Standard Version*), 233 times in the New Testament and 54 times in Matthew's Gospel. Jesus tells us to "go":

- "Go to the lost sheep ... "
- "Go and tell John ... "
- "Go and invite all you meet ... "
- "Go and make disciples ... "

Indeed, these are the last recorded words of Jesus in Matthew's Gospel:

Then Jesus came to them and said, "All authority in heaven and on earth has been given to me. Therefore go and make disciples of all nations, baptizing them in the name of the Father and of the Son and of the Holy Spirit, and teaching them to obey everything I have commanded you. And surely I am with you always, to the very end of the age" (Matthew 28:18-20).

Secondly, we tell people because people desperately need to hear the good news of Jesus Christ. If we were in the Sahara Desert and discovered an oasis, it would be extremely selfish not to tell the thirsty people around us where their thirst could be satisfied. Jesus is the only One who can satisfy the thirsty hearts of men and women.

"People out there are screaming for the truth."

Often the recognition of this thirst comes from surprising sources. The singer Sinead O'Connor said in an interview: "As a race we feel empty. This is because our spirituality has been wiped out and we don't know how to express ourselves. As a result we're encouraged to fill that gap with alcohol, drugs, sex, or money. People out there are screaming for the truth."

Thirdly, we tell others because, having discovered the Good News ourselves, we feel an urgent desire to pass it on. If we have received good news we want to tell others. When our first child was born, my wife, Pippa, gave me a list of about ten people to call. The first person I called was her mother. I told her that we had a son and that he and Pippa were well. I then tried calling my mother, but the phone was busy. The third person on the list was Pippa's sister. By the time I had telephoned her she had already heard the news from Pippa's mother and so had all the others on the list. My mother's phone had been busy because Pippa's mother was calling her with the news. Good news travels fast. I did not need to implore Pippa's mother to pass on the message. She was bursting to tell them all. When we appreciate what good news the Gospel is, we shall be bursting to tell others.

But how do we go about telling others? It seems to me that there are two opposite dangers. First, there is the danger of insensitivity. When I first became a Christian I fell into this. I was so excited about what had happened that I longed for everyone else to follow suit. After I had been a Christian for a few days I went to a party, determined to tell everyone. I saw a friend dancing and decided the first step was to make her realize her need. So I went up to her and said, "You look awful. You really need Jesus." She thought that I had gone mad. It was not the most effective way of telling someone the Good News! (However, she did later become a Christian—quite independently of me—and she is now my wife!)

The next time I went to a party, I decided to go well equipped. So I got hold of a number of booklets, Christian books on various issues, and a New Testament. I stuffed them into every pocket I could find. I asked a girl to dance. It was hard going with so many books in my pocket, so I asked if we could sit down. I soon brought the subject around to Christianity. For every question she asked, I was able to produce a book from my pocket on exactly that subject. Eventually she went away with an armful of books. The next day she was going to France and was reading one of the books I had given her on the boat. Suddenly she understood the truth of what Jesus had done for her and, turning to her neighbor, she said, "I have just become a Christian." She died in a riding accident at the age of twenty-one. It was wonderful that she had come to Christ before she died—even though I don't think I went about it in quite the right way.

If we charge around like a bull in a china shop, sooner or later we get hurt. Even if we approach the subject sensitively, we may still get hurt. When we do, we tend to withdraw. Certainly this was my experience. After a few years, I moved from the danger of insensitivity and fell into the opposite danger of fear.

If we charge around like a bull in a china shop, sooner or later we get hurt.

There was a time (ironically it was when I was in seminary) when I became fearful of even talking about Jesus to those who were not Christians. On one occasion, a group of us went from the school on a mission on the outskirts of Liverpool, to tell people the Good News. Each night we had supper with different people from the neighborhood. One night, my friend Rupert and I were sent to supper with a couple who were on the fringe of the church. To be more accurate, the wife was on the fringe and the husband was not a churchgoer. Halfway through the main course the husband asked me what we were doing up there. I stumbled, stammered, hesitated, and prevaricated. He kept on repeating the question. Eventually Rupert said straight out, "We have come here to tell people about Jesus." I felt deeply embarrassed and hoped the ground would swallow us all up! I realized how frozen with fear I had become and that I was afraid even to take the name of Jesus on my lips.

In order to avoid these dangers of insensitivity and fear, we need to realize that telling others about Jesus arises out of our own relationship with God. It is a natural part of that relationship. As we walk with God, it should be quite natural for us to talk to people about that relationship in cooperation with the Spirit of God.

I find it helpful to think of this subject under five headings, all beginning with the letter *P:* presence, persuasion, proclamation, power, and prayer.

PRESENCE

Jesus said to His disciples:

> You are the salt of the earth. But if the salt loses its saltiness, how can it be made salty again? It is no longer good for anything, except to be thrown out and trampled by men. You are the light of the world. A city on a hill cannot be hidden. Neither do people light a lamp and put it under a bowl. Instead they put it on its stand, and it gives light to everyone in the house. In the same way, let your light shine before men, that they may see your good deeds and praise your Father in heaven (Matthew 5:13-16).

Jesus calls us to have a wide-ranging influence ("the salt of the earth" and "the light of the world"). In order to exercise this influence, we need to be "in the world" (at work, in our neighborhoods, and among our family and friends). We must not withdraw into what John Stott calls our "elegant little ecclesiastical salt cellars." Yet we are called to be different—to live a radically different lifestyle from the world—so that we may be effective as salt and light in it.

We are called first to be salt. In centuries before refrigeration was invented, salt was used to keep meat wholesome and to prevent decay. We are called as Christians to stop society going bad. We do this by our words, as we speak out about moral standards and moral issues, and as we use our influence to bring about God's standards in society around us. We do it by our deeds as we play our part as citizens, aiming to create better social structures, working for justice, freedom, and dignity for the individual, and by helping to abolish discrimination. We do it also by our social action to help those who are casualties of our society. To this end, some Christians are called to get involved in local or national politics. Others are called to spend their lives like Mother Teresa and Jackie Pullinger "ministering *with* the poor" (to use Jackie Pullinger's expression). All of us are called to play a part in this to a greater or lesser extent.

Secondly, Jesus calls us to be light—to allow the light of Christ to shine through us. We do this by what Jesus calls "your good deeds"— everything that we do or say because we are Christians. Our good deeds can be summarized as loving our neighbors as ourselves.

Living out the Christian life is the most appropriate way of passing on the Good News to those who live in very close proximity to us.

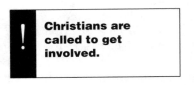

Christians are called to get involved.

This certainly applies to our family, colleagues at work, and roommates. If they know we are Christians, that fact alone puts them under a degree of pressure. To be continually speaking about our faith may backfire. They are more likely to be affected by genuine love and concern. At work people should notice our consistency, honesty, truthfulness, hard work, reliability, avoidance of gossip, and desire to encourage other people. At home, parents, family, and roommates will be influenced by our service to others, our patience, and our kindness, far more than by our words.

This is of great importance if one's husband or wife is not a Christian. Peter encouraged Christian wives that if any of them have husbands who "do not believe the word, they may be won over *without talk* by the behavior of their wives, when they see the purity and reverence of your lives" (1 Peter 3:1, italics mine).

Bruce and Geraldine Streather were married in December 1973. When Geraldine came to Christ in 1981, Bruce was not remotely interested. Bruce was a busy lawyer and an avid golfer: he used to play most weekends. He never came to church.

For ten years Geraldine prayed for him and lived out the Christian life in front of him. She did not put any pressure on him and did not engage in any arguments about her Christian faith. Over the years, Bruce was struck by her extraordinary kindness and consideration, especially to his mother whose cancer and related illnesses made her increasingly difficult. Eventually in 1991, she invited him to come to an *Alpha* dinner. Bruce came and decided to attend the next *Alpha Course*.

Geraldine wrote to me afterwards, saying, "I cried all the way home and prayed, telling God that as I had got Bruce to *Alpha*, He must do the rest. When Bruce returned from the first night of the course, I only asked him if he had enjoyed himself."

During week seven of the course, Bruce gave his life to Christ and by the end of the course he was the most enthusiastic Christian one could ever meet. I asked Geraldine what it was like living with him now. She replied, "It's a bit like living with Billy Graham!" Her letter continued:

187

He tells everyone about Jesus. Instead of trying not to mention Christianity in front of friends when Bruce was there, in case it harmed our marriage, at every dinner party he talks to people about God and I am left at the other end listening to what he is saying. It seems that all my prayers have been answered. Last March I told God that I was fed up with Bruce not being a Christian. I told him I didn't care what happened to our house or money as long as Bruce became a Christian. Life will never be the same again—thank God for that.

Being lights in the world does not just involve our lifestyle. It also involves our lips. Our family, our roommates, and our colleagues will eventually ask questions about our faith. It is often better to wait until they do. If we are asked, we should always be prepared to give an answer. Peter writes: "Always be prepared to give an answer to everyone who asks you to give the reason for the hope that you have. But do this with gentleness and respect"(1 Peter 3:15).

When we do get opportunities to speak, how do we go about it?

PERSUASION

Many people today have objections to the Christian faith or, at least, questions they want answered before they are ready to come to faith in Christ. They need to be persuaded of the truth. Paul was willing to try to persuade people. He regarded it as his duty out of love for them: "Since, then, we know what it is to fear the Lord, we try to *persuade* men" (2 Corinthians 5:11, italics mine).

When he went to Thessalonica Paul "reasoned," "explained," and "proved" from the Scriptures that the Christ had to suffer and rise from the dead ... Some of the Jews were persuaded" (Acts 17:2-4). In Corinth, while working on tents during the week, "every Sabbath he reasoned in the synagogue, trying to persuade Jews and Greeks" (Acts 18:4).

During the course of conversations about the Christian faith, people often will raise objections, and we need to be equipped to deal with these. On one occasion, Jesus was talking to a woman about the mess her life was in (John 4). Then He offered her eternal life. At that moment she raised a theological question about places of worship. He answered it, but quickly brought the conversation back to the essential issue. This is a good example for us to follow.

Usually when people raise theological questions and objections, they are genuinely looking for the answers. The most common questions that I get asked are, "Why does God allow suffering?" and "What about other religions?" But there are a whole range of other questions. These may be serious, and may require a serious answer. Sometimes, however, these questions can be a smoke screen to avoid the real issue. Such people are hesitant to become Christians not because of the theological objections but the moral ones. They are not willing to give their lives to Christ for fear of the change of lifestyle that Christianity will involve.

On the mission I mentioned earlier in the chapter, Rupert and I went to speak at a meeting about our Christian faith. After we had spoken, a university lecturer raised a large number of questions and objections. I didn't know where to begin to answer them all. Rupert simply asked, "If we could answer all your questions satisfactorily, would you become a Christian?" He replied, very honestly, "No." So there didn't seem a great deal of point in answering what for him were purely academic inquiries. But when the questions are genuine, reasoning, explaining, and proving form an important part of telling others about Jesus.

PROCLAMATION

The heart of telling others is the proclamation of the good news of Jesus Christ. It is announcing, communicating, and proclaiming the Christian faith to those outside the faith. This can be done in many ways. One of the most effective ways is bringing people to hear the Gospel explained by someone else. This can often be more advisable, especially in the early stages of our Christian lives, than trying to explain the Gospel ourselves.

Many who come to faith in Christ have lots of friends who have little or no connection with the church. This provides an excellent opportunity to say to these friends, as Jesus did on one occasion, "Come ... and you will see" (John 1:39). A woman in her twenties became a Christian and started attending church in London. On weekends, however, she would stay with her parents in Wiltshire. She then insisted on leaving them at 3:00 P.M. on Sunday afternoon in order to be in London in time for church. One Sunday evening she got stuck in a bad traffic jam and could not get to the evening service. She was so upset that she burst into tears. She went to see some friends who did not even know she had become a Christian. They asked her what was wrong. She answered through the tears, "I've missed church." They were totally mystified. The next Sunday they all came to see what they were missing! One of them came to Christ very shortly afterwards.

There is no greater privilege and no greater joy than enabling someone to find out about Jesus Christ. The former Archbishop of Canterbury, William Temple, wrote his commentary on John's Gospel while on his knees, asking God to speak to his heart. When he came to the words, "And he [Andrew] brought him [Simon] to Jesus" (John 1:42), Temple wrote a short but momentous sentence: "The greatest service that one man can render another."

 We can all do what Andrew did—we can bring someone to Jesus.

We don't hear much more about Andrew except that he was always bringing people to Jesus (John 6:8; 12:22). But Simon Peter, his brother, went on to be one of the greatest influences in the history of Christianity. We cannot all be Simon Peters, but we can all do what Andrew did—we can bring someone to Jesus.

Albert McMakin was a twenty-four-year-old farmer who had come to faith in Christ. He was so full of enthusiasm that he filled a truck with people and took them to a meeting to hear about Jesus. There was a good-looking farmer's son whom he especially wanted to get to a meeting, but this young man was hard to persuade. He was busy falling in and out of love with different girls and did not seem to be attracted to Christianity. Eventually, Albert McMakin managed to persuade him to come by asking him to drive the truck. When they arrived, Albert's guest decided to go in. He was spellbound and began to have thoughts he had never known before. He went back again and again until one night he went forward and gave his life to Jesus Christ. That man, the driver of the truck, was Billy Graham. The year was 1934. Since then Billy Graham has led thousands to faith in Jesus Christ. We cannot all be like Billy Graham, but we can all be like Albert McMakin—we can all bring our friends to Jesus.

He was spellbound and began to have thoughts he had never known before.

Sometimes we are given the opportunity to explain the Gospel ourselves. One good way of doing this is to tell the story of what has happened to us. We see a biblical model in Paul's testimony in Acts 26:9-23. It falls into three parts: he speaks about what he was like before (vss. 9-11), what it meant to meet Jesus (vss.. 12-18), and what it has meant for him since (vss. 19-23). When explaining what someone has to do to become a Christian, a framework can be helpful. The Gospel can be presented in many different ways. I have set out the method I use in a booklet called *Why Jesus?*. I then lead people in the prayer which you will find at the end of Chapter 3 (page 55)of this book, *Questions of Life.*

One man in our church told me recently about how he had come to Christ. He was going through difficulties in his business and had to go to the United States on a business trip. He was not feeling very happy as he rode in a taxi to the airport. On the dashboard of the taxi he noticed pictures of the taxi driver's children. He could not see the face of the driver, but he asked him about his family. He felt great love coming from the man. As the conversation went on, the taxi driver said to him, "I sense that you are not happy. If you believe in Christ it makes all the difference."

The businessman said to me, "Here was a man speaking with authority. I thought I was the one in authority. After all, I was paying." The taxi driver said to him eventually, "Don't you think it's time you settled all this by accepting Christ?" They arrived at the airport. For the first time the taxi driver turned round and the businessman saw his face; it was full of kindness. The driver said to him, "Why don't we pray? If you want Christ in your life, ask Him." They prayed together and the driver gave him a booklet about the Christian faith. The taxi driver was a modest, unassuming person who was there one moment and gone the next, but he had taken the opportunity to proclaim the good news of Jesus Christ. This changed the whole course of a man's life.

POWER

In the New Testament the proclamation of the Gospel is often accompanied by a demonstration of the power of God. Jesus came proclaiming: "The kingdom of God is near. Repent and believe the good news!" (Mark 1:15). Jesus went on to demonstrate the power of the Gospel by the expulsion of evil (Mark 1:21-28) and by healing the sick (Mark 1:29-34, 40-45).

Jesus told His disciples to do what He had been doing. He told them to do the works of the kingdom—"to heal the sick who are there" and to proclaim the Good News, and to tell them, "The kingdom of God is near you" (Luke 10:9). As we read on in the Gospels and Acts we see that that is what they did. Paul wrote to the Thessalonians: "Our gospel came to you not simply with words, but also with power" (1 Thessalonians 1:5).

Proclamation and demonstration go hand in hand. Often one leads to the other. On one occasion Peter and John were on their way to church. Outside was a man crippled from birth. He had been sitting there for years. He asked for money. Peter said, in effect, "I am sorry. I haven't got any money, but I will give you what I have. In the name of Jesus Christ of Nazareth, walk." He took his hand and helped him up. Instantly, the man jumped to his feet and began to walk. When he realized he was healed, he leapt and jumped and praised God (Acts 3:1-10).

Everyone knew that this man had been crippled for years, and a huge crowd gathered around. After the demonstration of the power of God came the proclamation of the Gospel. People were asking, "How did this happen?" Peter was able to tell them all about Jesus: "It is Jesus' name and the faith that comes through him that has given this complete healing to him, as you can all see" (Acts 3:16). In the next chapter we shall examine this area in more detail by looking at the nature of the kingdom of God and the place of healing in it.

PRAYER

We have already seen the importance that prayer had in the life of Jesus. While He was proclaiming and demonstrating the Gospel, He was also praying (Mark 1:35-37). Prayer is essential in the area of telling others the Good News.

We need to pray for blind eyes to be opened. Many people are blinded to the Gospel (2 Corinthians 4:4). They can see physically, but they cannot see the spiritual world. We need to pray that the Spirit of God will open the eyes of the blind so that they can understand the truth about Jesus.

Most of us find, when we come to faith in Christ, that somebody has been praying for us. It may be a member of the family, a god-parent, or a friend. Somebody, I suspect, in nearly every case, was praying that our eyes would be opened to see the truth. James Hudson Taylor, who founded the China Inland Mission, influenced

Most of us find when we come to faith that someone has been praying for us.

millions for Jesus Christ. He was brought up in Yorkshire, England, and became a rebellious teenager. One day, when his mother was away and his sister was out, he picked up a Christian book, intending to read the story and skip the moral. He curled up in the barn behind the house and began to read.

As he read, he was struck by the phrase, "the finished work of Christ." He thought Christianity to be a dreary struggle to pay off bad debts with good. He had long since abandoned the struggle. He owed too much. He sought simply to have a good time. This phrase broke open his mind to a sudden certainty that Christ, by His death on the cross, had already discharged this debt of sins: "And with this dawned the joyful conviction, as light was flashed into my soul by the Holy Spirit, that there was nothing in the world to be done but to fall down on one's knees and accepting this Savior and His Salvation, to praise Him for evermore." No Luther, Bunyan, or Wesley had a more complete sense of the rolling away of his burden, of light dismissing darkness, of rebirth and the close friendship of Christ, than did Hudson Taylor on that June afternoon in 1849 at the age of seventeen.

They prayed—not for protection, but for boldness.

Ten days later his mother came home. He ran to the door "to tell her I had such glad news to give." She replied as she hugged him, "I know, my boy. I have been rejoicing for a fortnight in the glad tidings you have to tell me." Hudson was amazed. She had been eighty miles away, and on the very day of the incident in the barn she had felt such an overwhelming desire to pray for Hudson that she had spent hours on her knees, and had arisen with the unshakable conviction that her prayers had been answered. He never forgot the importance of prayer.[51]

When a friend of mine, Ric, became a Christian he called a friend whom he knew to be a Christian as well, and told him what had happened. The friend replied, "I have been praying for you for four years." Ric then started to pray for one of his own friends, and within ten weeks he too became a Christian.

We need to pray for our friends. We also need to pray for ourselves. When we talk to people about Jesus, we may sometimes get a negative reaction. The temptation at the moment is to give up.

When Peter and John healed the crippled man and proclaimed the Gospel, they were arrested and threatened with dire consequences should they continue. At times, they got a decidedly negative reaction; but they did not give up. Rather, they prayed—not for protection, but for boldness in preaching the Gospel and for God to perform more signs and wonders through the name of Jesus (Acts 4:29-31).

It is vital for all of us as Christians to persevere in telling others about Jesus—by our presence, persuasion, proclamation, power, and prayer. If we do, over the course of a lifetime we shall see many lives changed.

During the war a man was shot and lay dying in the trenches. A friend leaned over to him and said, "Is there anything I can do for you?"

He replied, "No, I am dying."

"Is there anyone I can send a message to for you?"

"Yes, you can send a message to this man. Tell him that in my last minutes what he taught me as a child is helping me to die."

The man was the soldier's old Sunday school teacher. When the message got back to him, he said, "God forgive me. I gave up Sunday school teaching years ago because I thought I was getting nowhere. I thought it was no use."

When we tell people about Jesus, it is never no use. For the Gospel "is the power of God for the salvation of everyone who believes" (Romans 1:16).

13 | Does God Heal Today?

A few years ago, a young Japanese woman asked my wife and me to pray for her back problem to be healed. We placed our hands on her and asked God to heal her. After that, I tried to avoid bumping into her because I was not sure how to explain to her why she had not been healed. One day she came around the corner and I could not avoid her. I thought it only polite to ask the dreaded question, "How is your back?"

"Oh," she replied, "it was completely healed after you prayed."

I don't know why I was so surprised, but I was.

When John Wimber came to our church with a team from his church (the Vineyard Christian Fellowship), he preached one Sunday on the subject of healing. On Monday he came to a gathering of leaders. There were about sixty or seventy of us in the room, and he spoke again about healing. We had heard talks on healing before, and felt quite happy about what he said on the subject—until he said we were going to break for coffee and then have a "workshop." We were now on unfamiliar ground. John Wimber said that his team had had some twelve "words of knowledge" about the people in the room. He told us that by a "word of knowledge" (1 Corinthians 12:8 *King James Version*) he meant a supernatural revelation of facts concerning a person or a situation that is not learned by the efforts of the natural mind, but is made known by the Spirit of God. This may be in the form of a picture, a word seen or heard in the mind, or a feeling experienced physically. He then gave a whole list of them and said that he was going to invite people to come forward to be prayed for. I, for one, was most skeptical about the whole event.

However, one by one the people responded; some of the descriptions were quite detailed. My recollection is that one of them was for "a man who had injured his back chopping wood when he was fourteen." The level of faith in the room began to rise. Every word of knowledge was responded to. One of them concerned sterility. We all knew each other well and felt sure that this was not applicable to anyone in the group. However, a woman who had been unable to conceive bravely went forward. She was prayed for and had her first of five children exactly nine months later!

My attitude during that evening reflects the fear and skepticism many of us in the twentieth century bring to the subject of healing. I decided to reread the Bible to try to understand what it said about healing. Of course God heals with the cooperation of doctors, nurses and the whole medical profession. Their skills are God-given. The incarnation tells us that we must not drive a wedge between the human and the divine. Nevertheless, the more I looked, the more convinced I became that we should also expect God to heal directly and miraculously today.

HEALING IN THE BIBLE

In the Old Testament

In the Old Testament we find God's promises to bring healing and health to His people if they obey Him (for example, see Exodus 23:25, 26; Deuteronomy 28; Psalm 41). Indeed, it is in God's character to heal, for He says, "I am the Lord, who heals you" (Exodus 15:26). We also find several examples of miraculous healing (1 Kings 13:6; 2 Kings 4:8-37; Isaiah 38).

One of the most striking examples is the healing of Naaman, the commander of the army of the King of Aram. Naaman had leprosy.

200

God healed him after he had reluctantly dipped himself seven times in the Jordan River. "His flesh was restored and became clean like that of a young boy" (2 Kings 5:14), and he recognized the God of Israel to be the only true God. Elisha, who had instructed him, refused the payment that Naaman offered (although his servant Gehazi made the fatal mistake of trying, deceitfully, to get money for himself as a result of the healing).

We see, first, from this story that healing can have a remarkable effect on a person's life—not just physically, but also in their relationship with God. Healing and faith can go hand in hand. Secondly, if God acted in this way in the Old Testament, when there were only glimpses of the kingdom of God and the outpouring of the Spirit, we can confidently expect that He will do so, even more, now that Jesus has inaugurated the kingdom of God and the age of the Spirit.

In the New Testament

The first recorded words of Jesus in Mark's Gospel are, "The time has come … The kingdom of God is near. Repent and believe the good news!" (Mark 1:15).

The teachings of Jesus. The theme of the kingdom of God is central to the ministry of Jesus. The expressions "the kingdom of God" and "the kingdom of heaven" are used more than eighty-two times, although the latter is confined to Matthew's Gospel. The two terms are synonymous. "Heaven" was a common Jewish expression for referring to God without mentioning the divine name. The Jewish background to Matthew's Gospel, as opposed to the Gentile orientation of Luke and Mark, probably explains the different use.

The Greek word for "kingdom," *basileia*, is a translation of the Aramaic *malkuth*, which was in all probability the expression that Jesus used. It means not only "kingdom" in the sense of a political or geographical realm, but also carries the notion of activity—the activity of ruling or reigning. Thus "the kingdom of God" means "the rule and reign of God."

In the teaching of Jesus, the kingdom of God has a future aspect, which will only be fulfilled with a decisive event at "the end of the age" (Matthew 13:49). For example, in one of the parables of the Kingdom, Jesus speaks of a coming harvest at the end of the age when "the Son of Man ... will weed out of his kingdom everything that causes sin and all who do evil ... Then the righteous will shine like the sun in the kingdom of their Father" (Matthew 13:24-43). The end of the age will come when Jesus returns. When He came the first time, He came in weakness; when He returns, He will come "with power and great glory" (Matthew 24:30).

History is moving towards this climax with the glorious coming of Jesus Christ (Matthew 25:31). In all, there are over three hundred references in the New Testament to the second coming of Christ. When He returns it will be obvious to all. History, as we know it, will end. There will be a universal resurrection and a Day of Judgment. For some (those who reject Christ), it will be a day of destruction (2 Thessalonians 1:8, 9); for others, it will be a day of receiving their inheritance in the kingdom of God (Matthew 25:34). There will be a new heaven and a new earth (2 Peter 3:13; Revelation 21:1). Jesus Himself will be there (Revelation 21:22, 23) and so will all who love and obey Him. It will be a place of intense happiness that goes on forever (1 Corinthians 2:9). We shall have new bodies that are imperishable and glorious (1 Corinthians 15:42, 43). There will be no more death or mourning or crying or pain (Revelation 21:4). All who believe will be totally healed on that day.

On the other hand, there is a present aspect to the kingdom of God in the teaching and activity of Jesus. We see the signs, the dawning, the budding of the approaching Kingdom. Jesus told the Pharisees, "The kingdom of God is within you" (Luke 17:20, 21). In His parable of the hidden treasure and the pearl (Matthew 13:44-46),

Jesus suggests that the Kingdom is something that can be discovered and experienced in this age. Throughout the Gospels, it is clear Jesus saw His ministry as the fulfillment of the Old Testament promises in history. In the synagogue at Nazareth, Jesus read the prophecy from Isaiah 61:1, 2 and asserted, "Today this scripture is fulfilled in your hearing" (Luke 4:21). He went on to demonstrate this present reality of the Kingdom by all that He did during His ministry, in the forgiveness of sins, the suppression of evil, and the healing of the sick.

The Kingdom is both "now" and "not yet." The Jewish expectation was that the Messiah would immediately inaugurate a completed Kingdom, as shown in the diagram below:

THIS AGE | **AGE TO COME**

Jesus' teaching was a modification of this and can be summarized in the diagram below:

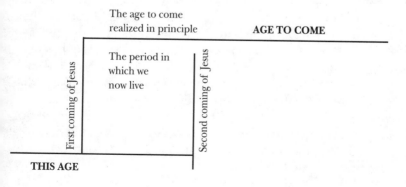

The age to come
realized in principle   **AGE TO COME**

First coming of Jesus

The period in
which we
now live

Second coming of Jesus

THIS AGE

We live between the times, when the age to come has broken into history. The old age goes on, but the powers of the new era have erupted into this age. The future kingdom has broken into history. Jesus preached the kingdom of God. He also demonstrated its breaking into history by healing the sick, raising the dead, and driving out demons.

The commissions of Jesus. A quarter of the Gospels is concerned with healing. Although Jesus did not heal all in Judea who were sick, we often read of Him healing either individuals or groups of people (for instance, Matthew 4:23; 9:35; Mark 6:56; Luke 4:40; 6:19; 9:11). It was part of the normal activity of the Kingdom.

Not only did Jesus have a healing ministry Himself, but He commissioned His disciples to do the same. First, He commissioned the twelve. This is clearly set out in Matthew's Gospel. Matthew tells us that "Jesus went throughout Galilee, teaching in their synagogues, preaching the good news of the kingdom, and healing every disease and sickness among the people" (Matthew 4:23). Matthew then gives some of the teaching and preaching of Jesus in chapters 5–7 (the Sermon on the Mount), then nine miracles (mainly of healing). Matthew concludes with an almost exact repetition of Matthew 4:23: "Jesus went through all the towns and villages, teaching in their synagogues, preaching the good news of the kingdom and healing every disease and sickness" (Matthew 9:35). Matthew uses a literary device of repetition known as an *inclusio.* This was used instead of punctuation and breaking up of the text with paragraphs to indicate the beginning and end of a section.

Having shown what Jesus Himself did, Matthew then tells us that

He told them to go out and preach the same message.

Jesus sent the twelve out to do the same. He told them to go out and preach the same message: "'The kingdom of heaven is near.' Heal the sick, raise the dead, cleanse those who have leprosy, drive out demons" (Matthew 10:8).

Nor was it only the twelve to whom He gave this commission. He also appointed a further group of seventy-two. He told them to go out and "heal the sick ... and tell them, 'The kingdom of God is near you'" (Luke 10:9). They returned with joy and said, "Lord, even the demons submit to us in your name" (vs. 17).

Nor were His commissions confined to the twelve and the seventy-two. Jesus expected *all* His disciples to do the same. He told His disciples to "go and make disciples of all nations ... teaching them to obey *everything* I have commanded you" (Matthew 28:18-20, italics mine). He did not say, "Everything except, of course, healing."

We find the same in the longer ending of Mark's Gospel. (The most reliable ancient manuscripts do not include Mark 16:9-20, but these verses still show us what the early church understood Jesus' commission to be.) Jesus said, "'Go into all the world and preach the good news to all creation ...

Jesus expected *all* His disciples to do the same.

and these signs will accompany *those who believe*: In my name they will drive out demons ... they will place their hands on sick people, and they will get well' ... Then the disciples went out and preached everywhere, and the Lord worked with them and confirmed his word by the signs that accompanied it" (Mark 16:15-20, italics mine). Jesus says, "These signs will accompany those who believe"—that is to say, those who believe in Jesus Christ, which means all Christians.

John's Gospel is also the same. Jesus said, in the context of miracles, "Anyone who has faith in me will do what I have been doing. He will do even greater things than these, because I am going to the Father" (John 14:12). Clearly no one has performed miracles of greater quality than Jesus, but there has been a greater quantity since Jesus returned to the Father. He has not ceased to perform miracles, but He now uses weak and imperfect human beings. Again it is "anyone who has faith in me." That is you and me. These commands and promises are not restricted to a special category of Christians.

Jesus healed; He told His disciples to do the same and they did so. In the Book of Acts we see the working out of this commission. The disciples not only continued to preach and teach, but also to heal the sick, raise the dead, and cast out demons (Acts 3:1-10; 4:1-12; 5:12-16; 8:5-13; 9:32-43; 14:3, 8-10; 19:11, 12; 20:9-12; 28:8, 9). It is clear from 1 Corinthians 12–14 that Paul did not believe that such abilities were confined to the apostles. Likewise, the writer to the Hebrews says that God testified to His message by "signs, wonders and various miracles, and gifts of the Holy Spirit" (Hebrews 2:4).

> **!** **Healing is one of the signs of the kingdom inaugurated by Jesus Christ.**

Nowhere in the Bible does it say that healing was confined to any particular period of history. On the contrary, healing is one of the signs of the Kingdom which was inaugurated by Jesus Christ and continues to this day. Hence we should expect God to continue to heal miraculously today as part of His Kingdom activity.

HEALING IN CHURCH HISTORY

In her book *Christian Healing* Evelyn Frost examined in detail passages of early church writers, such as Quadratus, Justin Martyr, Theophilus of Antioch, Irenaeus, Tertullian and Origen, and concluded that healing formed a normal part of the activity of the early church.

Irenaeus (about 130-200 A.D.), who was Bishop of Lyons and one of the theologians of the early church, wrote:

> Those who are in truth his disciples, receiving grace from him, do in his name perform [miracles], so as to promote the welfare of other men, according to the gift which each one has received from him. For some do certainly and truly drive out devils, so that those who have thus been cleansed from evil spirits frequently both believe [in Christ], and join themselves to the church. Others have foreknowledge of things to come: they see visions, and utter prophetic expressions. Others still, heal the sick by laying their hands upon them and they are made whole. Yea, moreover, as I have said, the dead have been raised up, and remain among us for many years.[52]

Origen (about 185-254 A.D.), another theologian, biblical scholar, and writer of the early church, said of Christians: "They expel evil spirits, and perform many cures, and foresee certain events ... the name of Jesus ... can take away diseases."

Two hundred years later there was still an expectation that God would heal people directly. Augustine of Hippo (354-430 A.D.), whom many regard as the greatest theologian of the first four centuries, says in his book *The City of God*, "even now miracles are wrought in the name of Christ." He cites the example of a blind man's sight restored in Milan, when Augustine was there. He then describes the cure of a man he was staying with, called Innocentius. Innocentius was being treated by the doctors for fistulas, of which he had "a large number intricately seated in the rectum!" He had undergone one very painful operation. It was not thought that he would survive another operation. While believers were praying for him he was cast down to the ground as if someone had hurled him violently to the earth, groaning and sobbing, his whole body shaking so that he could not speak. The dreaded day for the next operation came. "The surgeons arrived … the frightful instruments are produced … the part is bared; the surgeon … with knife in hand, eagerly looks for the sinus that is to be cut. He searches for it with his eyes; he feels for it with his finger; he applies every kind of scrutiny." He found a perfectly healed wound. "No words of mine can describe the joy, and praise, and thanksgiving to the merciful and almighty God which was poured from the lips of all, with tears and gladness. Let the scene be imagined rather than described!"

Next Augustine described the healing of Innocentia—a devout woman of the highest rank in the state—who was healed of what the doctors described as incurable breast cancer. The doctor was curious to find out how she had been healed. When she told him that Jesus had healed her, he was furious and said, "I thought you would make some great discovery to me." Shuddering at the indifference, she quickly replied, "What great thing was it for Christ to heal a cancer, who raised one who had been four days dead?"

All the way through church history God has continued to heal people directly.

Augustine goes on to tell of a doctor with gout who was healed in the "very act of baptism" and an old comedian who was also cured at baptism, not only of paralysis, but also of a hernia. Augustine says he knows of so many miraculous healings that he says at one point, "What am I to do? I am so pressed by the promise of finishing this work, that I cannot record all the miracles I know … even now, therefore many miracles are wrought, the same God, who wrought those we read of, still performing them, by whom he will and as he will."

All the way through church history God has continued to heal people directly. There has never been a time when healing has died out—right up to the present day.

Edward Gibbon (1737-1794), the English rationalist, historian, and scholar, best known as the author of *The History of the Decline and Fall of the Roman Empire*, lists five causes for the remarkable and rapid growth of Christianity. One of these is "the miraculous powers of the primitive Church." He says, "The Christian Church, from the time of the apostles and their first disciples has claimed an uninterrupted succession of miraculous powers, the gift of tongues, of vision and of prophecy, the power of expelling demons, of healing the sick and of raising the dead." Gibbon goes on to point out the inconsistency of his own day when "a latent, and even involuntary, scepticism adheres to the most pious dispositions." By contrast to the early church, Gibbon writes that in the church of his day "admission of supernatural truths is much less an active consent than a cold and placid acquiescence. Accustomed long since to observe and to respect the invariable order of Nature, our reason, or at least our imagination, is not sufficiently prepared to sustain the visible action of the Deity." The same could be said even more so of our own day.

HEALING TODAY

God is still healing people today. There are so many wonderful stories of God healing that it is difficult to know which to give as an example. Ajay Gohill told his story at a recent baptism and confirmation service at our church. He was born in Kenya and went to England in 1971. He had been brought up as a Hindu and worked in his family business as a newsagent in Neasden. At the age of twenty-one he contracted erythrodermic psoriasis, a chronic skin disease. His weight dropped from 161 to 105 pounds. He was treated all over the world—in the United States, Germany, Switzerland, Israel, and all over England. He said that he spent eighty percent of his earnings on trying to find a cure. He took strong drugs that affected his liver. Eventually, he had to give up his job. The disease was all over his body from head to toe. He was so horrible to look at that he could

209

not go swimming or even wear a T-shirt. He lost all his friends. His wife and son left him. He wanted to die. On August 20, 1987, he was in a wheelchair in the Elizabeth Ward of St. Thomas's Hospital. He spent over seven weeks in the hospital receiving various kinds of treatments. On October 14, he was lying in his bed and wanted to die. He cried out, "God, if you are watching, let me die—I am sorry if I have done something wrong." He said that as he prayed he "felt a presence." He looked in his locker and pulled out a *Good News Bible*. He opened it at random and read Psalm 38:

> O Lord, don't punish me in your anger! You have wounded me with your arrows; you have struck me down. Because of your anger, I am in great pain; my whole body is diseased because of my sins. I am drowning in the flood of my sins; they are a burden too heavy to bear. Because I have been foolish, my sores stink and rot. I am bowed down, I am crushed; I mourn all day long. I am burning with fever and I am near to death. I am worn out and utterly crushed; my heart is troubled, and I groan with pain. O Lord, you know what I long for; you hear all my groans. My heart is pounding, my strength is gone, and my eyes have lost their brightness. My friends and neighbors will not come near me, because of my sores; even my family keeps away from me …. Do not abandon me, O Lord; do not stay away, my God! Help me now, O Lord my savior! (Psalm 38:1-11, 21, 22, *Good News Bible*).

Each and every verse seemed relevant to Gohill. He prayed for God to heal him and fell into a deep sleep. When he awoke the next morning everything looked new. He went to the bathroom and relaxed in a bath. As he looked at the bathwater, he saw his skin had lifted off and was floating in the bath. He called the nurses in and told them that God was healing him. All his skin was new like a baby's. He had been totally healed. Since then he has been reunited with his son. He says that the inner healing that has taken place in his life is even greater than the physical healing. He says, "Every day I live for Jesus. I am his servant today."

God is a God who heals. The Greek word that means "I save" also means "I heal." God is concerned not just about our spiritual salvation, but also about our whole being. One day we shall have a new perfect body. In this life we never reach perfection. When God heals someone miraculously today we get a glimpse of the future when the final redemption of our bodies will take place (Romans 8:23). Not everyone we pray for will necessarily be healed. Of course, no human being can ultimately avoid death. Our bodies are decaying. At some point it may be right to prepare a person for death rather than praying for their healing. Indeed, the love and concern shown to dying people by the Hospice movement and others, give dignity to the terminally ill and is another outworking of Jesus' commission to care for the sick. So we need to be sensitive to the guidance of the Holy Spirit.

> **When God heals someone miraculously today we get a glimpse of the future.**

This should not discourage us from praying for people to be healed. The more we pray for, the more we shall see healed. Those who are not healed usually speak of the blessing of being prayed for—provided they are prayed for with love and sensitivity. I remember a group of us in seminary praying for a man with a bad back. I don't think he was healed, but he said to me afterwards, "This is the first time since I have been in seminary that I felt anyone cared." Another man said to me recently that, although he had not been healed when he was prayed for, he had had his greatest experience ever of the Spirit of God, and his life has been transformed.

Some are given special gifts of healing (1 Corinthians 12:9). Today, around the world, we find examples of those with an extraordinary gift of healing. This does not mean that we can leave it all to

211

them. The commission to heal is for all of us. Just as we do not all have the gift of evangelism, but we are all called to tell others about Jesus, so we do not all have the gift of healing, but we are all called to pray for the sick.

How in practice do we go about praying for the sick? It is vital to remember that it is God who heals, not us. There is no technique involved. We pray with love and simplicity. The motivation of Jesus was His compassion for people (Mark 1:41; Matthew 9:36). If we love people we will always treat them with respect and dignity. If we believe it is Jesus who heals we will pray with simplicity, because it is not our prayer but the power of God that brings healing.

Here is a simple pattern:

Where does it hurt?

We ask the person who wants prayer for healing what is wrong and what he or she would like us to pray for.

Why does the person have this condition?

Of course, a leg broken in a car accident will be obvious, but at other times we may need to ask God to show us if there is a root cause to the problem. One woman in our congregation had developed a backache with pain in her left hip. This interfered with sleep, movement, and work. The doctor prescribed pills for arthritis. She asked for prayer one evening. The young woman who was praying for her said that the word "forgiveness" had come to her mind. After a struggle the woman was able to forgive someone who was continually troubling her, and she was partially healed. She was totally healed at the moment she mailed a forgiving letter to her friend.

How do I pray?

The New Testament gives various models for prayer we may follow.

They are all simple. Sometimes we pray for God to heal in the name of Jesus and we ask the Holy Spirit to come on the person. Or prayer is accompanied by anointing with oil (James 5:14). More often it is accompanied by the laying on of hands (Luke 4:40).

How does the person feel?

After we have prayed we usually ask the person what he or she is experiencing. Sometimes the person feels nothing, in which case we continue to pray. At other times the person feels that he or she is healed, although time alone will tell. On other occasions the person feels better but is not totally healed, in which case we continue as Jesus did with the blind man (Mark 8:22-25). We continue praying until we feel it is right to stop.

What next?

After praying for healing it is important to reassure people of God's love for them regardless of whether they are healed or not, and to give them the liberty to come back and be prayed for again. We must avoid putting burdens on people, such as suggesting that it is a lack of faith that has prevented healing from taking place. We always encourage people to go on praying and to ensure that their lives are rooted in the healing community of the church—which is the place where long-term healing often occurs.

Finally, it is important to persist in praying for people to be healed. It is easy to get discouraged, especially if we do not see immediate, dramatic results. We continue because of our obedience to the calling and commission from Jesus Christ to preach the Kingdom and to demonstrate its coming by, among other things, healing the sick. If we persist over the years we will see God healing people.

I was once asked to visit a woman in the hospital. She was in her thirties, had three children and was pregnant with a fourth. Her common-law husband had left her and she was on her own. Her

213

third child, who had Down's syndrome, had a hole in his heart that had been operated on. The operation had not been a success and, not unnaturally, the medical staff wanted to turn the machines off.

They knew they had seen God's power in healing.

Three times they asked her if they could turn the machines off and let the baby die. She had said no; she wanted to try one last thing. She wanted someone to pray for him. So I came, and she told me that she didn't believe in God, but she showed me her son. He had tubes all over him and his body was bruised and swollen. She said that the doctors had indicated that even if he recovered he would have brain damage because his heart had stopped for such a long time. She said, "Will you pray?" So I prayed in the name of Jesus for God to heal him. Then I explained to her how she could give her life to Jesus Christ and she did that. I left, but returned two days later. She came running out the moment she saw me. She said, "I've been trying to get hold of you: something amazing has happened. The night after you prayed he completely turned the corner. He has recovered." Within a few days he had gone home. I tried to keep in contact with her, but I didn't know where she lived. She kept leaving messages on my phone.

About six months later I was in the elevator in another hospital and saw a mother and child. I did not recognize them at first. The woman said, "Are you Nicky?" I said, "Yes." She said, "That is the little boy you prayed for. It is amazing. Not only has he recovered from the operation, but his hearing, which was bad beforehand, is better. He still has Down's syndrome, but he is much better than he was before."

Since then I have presided at two funerals for other members of that family. At each of them people have come up to me, none of them churchgoers, saying, "You were the person who prayed for

Craig to be healed and God healed him." They all believed that God healed him, because they knew that he was dying. The change in Vivienne, the child's mother, had also made a deep impression on them. She was so changed after coming to Christ that she decided to marry the person with whom she was living. He had come back to her after seeing the change in her life. They are now married and she is transformed. At the second funeral, Vivienne went around to all the relatives and friends saying, "I didn't believe, but now I do believe." Not long afterwards, Craig's uncle and aunt came to church, sat in the front row, and gave their lives to Jesus Christ. They did so because they knew they had seen God's power in healing.

14 What About the Church?

Abraham Lincoln said, "If all the people who fell asleep in church on Sunday morning were laid out end to end … they would be a great deal more comfortable." Hard pews, unsingable tunes, enforced silence, and excruciating boredom are just a few ingredients that make up the common image of church. It is seen as an experience through which to grit one's teeth stoically until the aroma of gravy brightens up the prospects of the day. A pastor was taking a small boy around his church and showing him the memorials. "These are the names of those who died in the Services." The boy asked, "Did they die at the morning service or at the evening service?"

Some associate the word "church" with the clergy. Somebody who is entering the ordained ministry is said to be "going into the church." Those embarking on such a career are often viewed with suspicion, and the assumption is made that they are absolutely incapable of doing anything else. Hence a recent advertisement in a church newspaper: "Are you forty-five and getting nowhere? Why not consider the Christian ministry?" Clergy are sometimes perceived as: "Six days invisible, one day incomprehensible!"

Others associate the word "church" with a particular denomination. For example, the Episcopalians, the Roman Catholics, the Baptists, or the Methodists. Still others associate the word "church" with church buildings. They assume that to be a clergyman you must be interested in church architecture, and when they go on vacation they send their pastors pictures of local church buildings. I heard one clergyman imploring his congregation not to send him postcards of churches, telling them he had little interest in church architecture!

Some check off "church" on their list of yearly duties, somewhere between visiting Great Aunt Edna in Chicago and making a cake for the town festival. The attitude of others is summed up in a ditty:

> So when I've nothing else to do,
> I think I'll pay a visit,
> So when at last I'm carried in,
> The Lord won't say, "Who is it?"

Some of these views may contain an element of truth. However, many Christians are seeking to bury this image of the church because it is wholly inadequate when compared to the picture of the church in the New Testament. Many churches are now creating a wonderfully warm and outward-going Christian family that is much closer to the biblical picture. In the New Testament there are over one hundred images or analogies of the church. In this chapter I want to look at five central to the understanding of the church.

THE PEOPLE OF GOD

The church is made up of people. The Greek word for church, *ekklesia*, means "an assembly" or "gathering of people." Sometimes the New Testament refers to the universal church (see Ephesians 3:10, 21; 5:23, 25, 27, 29, 32). The universal church consists of all those worldwide and down the ages who profess or have professed the name of Christ.

Baptism is a visible mark of being a member of the church. It is also a visible sign of what it means to be a Christian. It signifies cleansing from sin (1 Corinthians 6:11), dying and rising with Christ to a new life (Romans 6:3-5; Colossians 2:12), and the living water that the Holy Spirit brings to our lives (1 Corinthians 12:13). Jesus Himself commanded His followers to go and make disciples and to baptize them (Matthew 28:19).

The universal Christian church is vast. According to the *Encyclopedia Britannica*, it has nearly 1.9 billion adherents in 270 countries, consisting of 34 percent of the world population. In many parts of the world, where there are extreme and oppressive regimes, the church is persecuted. In these parts the church is mainly underground but, by all accounts, very strong. In the Third World it is growing rapidly. In some countries, such as Kenya, it is estimated that eighty percent of the population are now professed Christians.

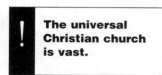

The universal Christian church is vast.

On the other hand, in the free world the church has largely been in decline. In the United States, five major mainline denominations saw a severe decline in church membership and volunteer involvement during the 1980s. At one time the West was sending missionaries to the Third World. However, I remember that when I was in Cambridge, three Ugandan missionaries came there to preach the Gospel. It struck me then how much the world had changed in the last 150 years, and that England needed missionaries as much as anywhere else.

In the New Testament, Paul speaks of local churches, for example the "Galatian churches" (1 Corinthians 16:1), "the churches in the province of Asia" (1 Corinthians 16:19) and "all the churches of Christ" (Romans 16:16). Even those local churches seem at times to have broken down into smaller gatherings that met in homes (Romans 16:5; 1 Corinthians 16:19).

The Bible mentions three types of gatherings: the large, the medium-sized, and the small. Church growth writers sometimes speak of a three-tier structure of celebration, congregation, and cell. All three are important and complement each other.

Celebration. The celebration is a large gathering of Christians. This may take place every Sunday in big churches or when a number of small churches come together for worship. In the Old Testament, the people of God came together for special celebrations with a festive atmosphere at Passover or at the New Year. Today, large gatherings of Christians provide inspiration. Through them many can recapture a vision of the greatness of God and a profound sense of worship. These gatherings of hundreds of Christians together can restore confidence to those who have felt isolated and provide a visible presence of the church in the community. However, on their own such gatherings are not enough. They are not places where Christian friendships can easily develop.

Congregation. The congregation, in this sense, is a medium-sized gathering. The size makes it possible to know most people and be known by most. It is a place where lasting Christian friendships can be made. It is also a place where the gifts and ministries of the Spirit can be exercised in an atmosphere of love and acceptance, where people are free to risk making mistakes. The congregation is a place where individuals can learn, for example, to give talks, lead worship, pray for the sick, develop the gift of prophecy, and pray out loud.

Cell. The third level of meeting is the cell, which we call the small group. These groups consist of two to twelve people who gather to study the Bible and pray together. It is in these groups that the closest friendships in the church are made. They are characterized by confidentiality (we can speak openly without fear of gossip), intimacy (we can speak about what really matters in our lives), and accountability (we are willing to listen to and learn from one another).

It is a place where lasting Christian friendships can be made.

THE FAMILY OF GOD

When we receive Jesus Christ into our lives, we become children of God (John 1:12). This is what gives the church its unity. We have God as our Father, Jesus Christ as our Savior, and the Holy Spirit as our indweller. We all belong to one family. Although brothers and sisters may squabble and fall out or not see each other for long periods of time, they still remain brothers and sisters. Nothing can end that relationship. So the church is one, even though it often appears divided.

This does not mean that we settle for disunity. Jesus prayed for His followers "that they may be one" (John 17:11). Paul says, "Make every effort to keep the unity of the Spirit" (Ephesians 4:3). Like a divided family we should always strive for reconciliation. The incarnation demands a visible expression of our invisible unity. Of course, this unity should not be achieved at the expense of truth but, as the Medieval writer Rupertus Meldenius put it, "On the necessary points, unity; on the questionable points, liberty; in everything, love."

At every level we should seek unity—in the small group, congregation, and celebration; within our denomination and between denominations. This unity is brought about as theologians and church leaders get together to debate and work through theological differences. But it is also achieved, often more effectively, by ordinary Christians getting together to worship and work together. The nearer we come to Christ, the nearer we come together. David Watson used a striking illustration. He said:

> When you travel by air and the plane lifts off the ground, the walls and hedges which may seem large and impressive at ground level, at once lose their significance. In the same way, when the power of the Holy Spirit lifts us up together into the conscious realisation of the presence of Jesus, the barriers between us become unimportant. Seated with Christ in the heavenly places, the differences between Christians can often seem petty and marginal.[53]

Since we have the same Father, we are brothers and sisters and are all called to love one another. John puts it very clearly:

> If anyone says, "I love God," yet hates his brother, he is a liar. For anyone who does not love his brother, whom he has seen, cannot love God, whom he has not seen. And he has given us this command: Whoever loves God must also love his brother. Everyone who believes that Jesus is the Christ is born of God, and everyone who loves the father loves his child as well (1 John 4:20–5:1).

The Pope's personal preacher, Father Raniero Cantalamessa, addressing a gathering of thousands from many different denominations said, "When Christians quarrel we say to God: 'Choose between us and them.' But the Father loves *all* his children. We should say, 'We accept as our brothers all those whom you receive as your children.'"

We are called to fellowship with one another. The Greek word *koinonia* means "having in common" or "sharing." It is the word used for the marital relationship, the most intimate between human beings. Our fellowship is with God (Father, Son, and Holy Spirit—1 John 1:3; 2 Corinthians 13:14) and with one another (1 John 1:7). Christian fellowship cuts across race, color, education, background, and every other cultural barrier. There is a level of friendship in the church that I have certainly never experienced outside the church.

The nearer we come to Christ, the nearer we come together.

John Wesley said, "The New Testament knows nothing of solitary religion." We are called to fellowship with one another. It is not an optional extra. There are two things we simply cannot do alone. We cannot marry alone and we cannot be a Christian alone. Professor C.E.B. Cranfield put it like this: "The freelance Christian, who would be a Christian but is too superior to belong to the visible Church upon earth in one of its forms, is simply a contradiction in terms."

The writer of Hebrews urges his readers, "Let us consider how we may spur one another on toward love and good deeds. Let us not give up meeting together, as some are in the habit of doing, but let us encourage one another—and all the more as you see the Day approaching" (Hebrews 10:24, 25). Often Christians lose their love for the Lord and their enthusiasm for their faith because they neglect fellowship.

One man who found himself in this position was visited by a wise old Christian. They sat in front of the coal fire in the sitting room. The old man never spoke, but he went to the coal fire and picked out a red-hot coal and put it on the hearth. He still said nothing. In a few minutes the coal had lost its glow. Then he picked it up and put it back in the fire. After a short time it began to glow again. The old man still said nothing at all but, as he got up to leave, the other man knew exactly why he had lost his fervor: a Christian out of fellowship is like a coal out of the fire. Martin Luther wrote in his diary, "At home in my house there is no warmth or vigor in one, but in the church when the multitude is gathered together, a fire is kindled in my heart and it breaks its way through."

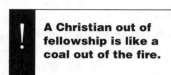
A Christian out of fellowship is like a coal out of the fire.

THE BODY OF CHRIST

Paul had been persecuting the Christian church when he encountered Jesus Christ on the road to Damascus. Jesus said to him, "Saul, Saul, why do you persecute *me*?" (Acts 9:4, italics mine). Paul had never met Jesus before so he must have realized that Jesus was saying that, in persecuting Christians, he was persecuting Jesus Himself. It may well be that from his encounter Paul realized that the church was, in effect, the body of Christ. "He calls the church Christ," wrote the sixteenth-century reformer, Calvin. We Christians are Christ to the world. As the old hymn says:

> He has no hands but our hands
> To do His work today;
> He has no feet but our feet
> To lead men in His way;
> He has no voice but our voice
> To tell men how He died;
> He has no help but our help
> To lead them to His side.

Unity

Paul develops this hymn's analogy in 1 Corinthians 12. The body is a unit (vs. 12), yet this unity does not mean uniformity. "Those who are members of one another become as diverse as the hand and the ear. That is why the worldlings are so monotonously alike compared with the almost fantastic variety of the saints. Obedience is the road to freedom, humility the road to pleasure, unity the road to personality."[54] There are many parts and they are all different with different kinds of gifts and different kinds of working (vss. 4-6).

Diversity

What then should our attitude be to other parts of the body of Christ?

Paul deals with two wrong attitudes. First, he speaks to those who feel inferior and who feel that they have nothing to offer. For example, Paul says the foot may feel inferior to the hand or the ear inferior to the eye (vss.. 14-19). Chrysostom, preaching in the fourth century, made a good comment when he said, "We are prone to envy."

It is easy to look round the church and feel inferior and therefore not needed. As a result we do nothing. In fact, we are all needed. God has given gifts "to each one" (vs. 7). The term "to each one" runs through 1 Corinthians 12 as a common thread. Each person has at least one gift, which is absolutely necessary for the proper functioning of the body. Unless each of us plays the part God has designed for us, the church will not be able to function as it should. In the following verses, Paul turns to those who feel superior (vss. 21-25) and are saying to others, "I don't need you." Again, Paul points out the folly of this position. A body without a foot is not as effective as it might be (see vs. 21). Often the parts that are unseen are even more important than those with a higher profile.

The right attitude recognizes that we are all in it together. We are all part of a team—each part affects the whole. From Plato onwards, the "I" has been the personality that gives unity to the body. We do not say, "My head has an ache." We say, "I have a headache." So it is with the body of Christ. "If one part suffers, every part suffers with it; if one part is honored, every part rejoices with it" (vs. 26).

Dependence

Every Christian is a part of the church. John Wimber was once approached by a member of his congregation who had met somebody in great need. After the Sunday service this man told John Wimber of his frustration in trying to get help. "This man needed a place to stay, food, and support while he gets on his feet and looks for a job," he said. "I am really frustrated. I tried telephoning the church office, but no one could see me and they couldn't help me. I finally ended up having to let him stay with me for the week! Don't you think the church should take care of people like this?" John Wimber thought for a moment and then said, "It looks like the church did."

As we saw in Chapter 8, the problem with the church is that for years it has either been pulpit-centered or altar-centered, according to our different traditions. In both situations the dominant role has been played by the minister or the priest. As Michael Green said, commenting on the spectacular spread of the Pentecostal churches in South America, "It is ... due to many causes, but not least to the fact that it is predominantly a lay church."[57]

A HOLY TEMPLE

The only church building the New Testament speaks about is a building made of people. Paul says that the Christians are "being built together to become a dwelling in which God lives by his Spirit" (Ephesians 2:22). Jesus is the chief cornerstone. He is the one who founded the church and around whom the church is built. The

foundations are the apostles and prophets and the result is a holy temple made of "living stones."

In the Old Testament the tabernacle (and later the temple) was central to Israel's worship. This was the place where people went to meet with God. At times His presence filled the temple (1 Kings 8:11) and especially the Holy of Holies. Access to His presence was strictly limited (see Hebrews 9).

Through His death on the cross for us, Jesus opened up access to the Father for all believers all the time. His presence is no longer confined to a physical temple; now He is present by His Spirit with all believers. His presence is especially sensed when Christians gather together (Matthew 18:20). His new temple is the church which is "a dwelling in which God lives by his Spirit."

Under the Old Covenant (before Jesus), access to the Father was through a priest (Greek word *hiereus*, Hebrews 4:14), who made sacrifices on behalf of believers. Now Jesus, our great high priest (*hiereus*), has made the supreme sacrifice of His own life on our behalf. No further sacrifices are necessary and no further priests are necessary. The only other time the word *hiereus* appears in the New Testament it is used to refer to all Christians being "a royal priesthood" (1 Peter 2:9). This is what the reformers called "the priesthood of all believers." All Christians are priests in the sense that we all have access to God, we can all represent men to God as we pray for others, and we all represent God to men as we go out into the world.

The word "priest" has another meaning. The English word "presbyter" (Greek *presbuteros*), which means "elder," became "preost" in old English and from this "priest." Priest, in this sense, is not a sacrificing priest like that of the Old Testament, but is a leader in the church. There are still priests (*presbuteroi*) today. Every Christian is a priest (in the *hiereus* sense) and every priest (*presbuteros*) is lay in the sense that he and all of us are part of the people of God.

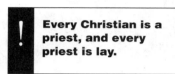

Every Christian is a priest, and every priest is lay.

There is no need for sacrificing priests today because there is no need for further sacrifices. Jesus "appeared once for all at the end of the ages to do away with sin by the sacrifice of himself" (Hebrews 9:26). We do not need to make further sacrifices for our sins; indeed we cannot. Rather, we need to be constantly reminded of His sacrifice for us. At the service of Holy Communion, sometimes called the Lord's Supper or the Eucharist, we remember His sacrifice with thanksgiving and partake of its benefits.

As we receive the bread and cup we look in four directions:

We look back with thanks

The bread and cup remind us of the broken body and shed blood of Jesus Christ on the cross. As we receive Communion we look back to the cross with thankfulness that He died for us so that our sins could be forgiven and our guilt removed (Matthew 26:26-28)

We look forward with anticipation

Jesus could have left us some other way to remember His death, but He chose to leave us a meal. A meal is often a way in which we celebrate great occasions. One day in heaven we are going to celebrate for eternity at "the wedding supper" of Jesus Christ (Revelation 19:9). The bread and cup are a foretaste of this (Luke 22:16; 1 Corinthians 11:26).

We look around at the Christian family

Sharing the bread and cup with other believers symbolizes our unity in Christ. "Because there is one loaf, we, who are many, are one body, for we all partake of the one loaf" (1 Corinthians 10:17). That is why we do not receive the bread and the wine on our own. Eating and drinking together in this way should not only remind us of our unity, it should strengthen that unity as we look around at our brothers and sisters, for each of whom Christ died.

We look up in expectation

The bread and wine represent the body and blood of Jesus. Jesus promised to be with us by His Spirit after His death, and especially wherever Christians meet together: "Where two or three come together in my name, there am I with them" (Matthew 18:20). So as we receive Communion we look up to Jesus with expectancy. In our experience, we have found that conversions, healing, and powerful encounters with the presence of Christ sometimes occur on such occasions.

THE BRIDE OF CHRIST

This is one of the most beautiful analogies of the church in the New Testament. Paul says when speaking of the husband and wife relationship: "This is a profound mystery—but I am talking about Christ and the church" (Ephesians 5:32).

The Old Testament speaks about God being a husband to Israel (Isaiah 54:1-8); in the New Testament Paul speaks about Christ being a husband to the church and the model of every human marriage relationship. So he tells husbands to love their wives "just as Christ loved the church and gave himself up for her to make her holy, cleansing her by the washing with water through the word, and to present her to himself as a radiant church, without stain or wrinkle or any other blemish, but holy and blameless" (Ephesians 5:25-27).

This picture of the holy and radiant church may not accord with the present condition of the church, but we get a glimpse of what Jesus intends for His church. One day Jesus will return in glory. In the Book of Revelation, John has a vision of the church, "the new Jerusalem, coming down out of heaven from God, prepared as a bride beautifully dressed for her husband" (Revelation 21:2). Today the church is small and weak. One day we shall see the church as Jesus intends it to be. In the meantime, we must try to bring our experiences as close as possible to the vision of the New Testament.

Our response to Christ's love for us should be one of love for Him. The way we show our love for Him is by living in holiness and purity—being a bride fit for Him and fulfilling His purpose for us. This is His intention for us. This is how His purposes for us will be fulfilled. We are to be changed and to be made beautiful until we are fit to be His bride.

Our response to Christ's love for us should be one of love for Him.

Moreover, His purpose for His church is that we "may declare the praises of him who called you out of darkness into his wonderful light" (1 Peter 2:9). Declaring His praises involves both worship and witness. Our worship is the expression of our love and reverence for

God with our whole beings—heart, mind, and bodies. This is the purpose for which we were made. As the Westminster catechism puts it, "The chief end of man is to glorify God and enjoy him for ever."

Our witness is our response of love towards other people. He has called us to tell others the Good News and draw them into His church—to declare His wonderful deeds to the people around us. In both our worship and our witness, we need to find a contemporary expression for eternal truths. God does not change; neither does the Gospel. We cannot change our doctrine or our message to suit passing fashions. But the way in which we worship and the way in which we communicate the Gospel must resonate with modern men and women. For many this will mean contemporary music and language.

If the church was closer to the New Testament images, church services would be far from dull and boring. Indeed, they should be very exciting—and sometimes are. The church is made up of the people who belong to God, bound together in love as a family, representing Christ to the world, with His presence in their midst, and loving their Lord as a bride loves the bridegroom, and being loved by Him as a bride is loved by the bridegroom. What a place to be—it should be near heaven on earth.

A young couple who had recently come to faith in Christ wrote:

We have been coming to church for a year now and it already feels like home. The atmosphere of love, friendship and excitement is impossible to find elsewhere. The joy of it far exceeds any evening at a pub, party or restaurant … I am shocked to say (although I continue to enjoy all three). Both of us find that Sunday's service and Wednesday's gathering are two high points of the week. At times, it feels like coming up for air, especially as by Wednesday it is easy to be drowning in the deep waters of working life! If we miss either, we feel somehow "diluted." Of course, we can keep talking to God together and alone, but I feel that the act of meeting together is the bellows that keep on fanning the flames of our faith.

15 How Can I Make the Most Of the Rest of My Life?

We only get one life. We might wish for more. D. H. Lawrence said, "If only one could have two lives. The first in which to make one's mistakes … and the second in which to profit by them." But there are no dress rehearsals for life; we are on stage immediately.

Even if we have made mistakes in the past, it is possible with God's help to make something of what is left. Paul tells us in Romans 12:1, 2 how we can do this:

> Therefore, I urge you, brothers, in view of God's mercy, to offer your bodies as living sacrifices, holy and pleasing to God—this is your spiritual act of worship. Do not conform any longer to the pattern of this world, but be transformed by the renewing of your mind. Then you will be able to test and approve what God's will is—his good, pleasing and perfect will.

WHAT SHOULD WE DO?

Break from the past

As Christians we are called to be different from the world around us. Paul writes, "Do not conform any longer to the pattern of this world" (by which he means the world that has shut God out). Or as J. B. Phillips translates this verse, "Don't let the world around you squeeze you into its own mold." This is not easy; there is a pressure to conform, to be like everybody else. It is very hard to be different.

A young police officer was taking his final exam at a police training college in north London. Here is one of the questions:

You are on patrol in outer London when an explosion occurs in a gas main in a nearby street. On investigation you find that a large hole has been blown in the footpath and there is an overturned van lying nearby. Inside the van there is a strong smell of alcohol. Both occupants—a man and a woman—are injured. You recognize the woman as the wife of your Divisional Inspector, who is at present away in the USA. A passing motorist stops to offer you assistance and you realize that he is a man who is wanted for armed robbery. Suddenly a man runs out of a nearby house, shouting that his wife is expecting a baby and that the shock of the explosion has made the birth imminent. Another man is crying for help, having been blown into an adjacent canal by the explosion, and he cannot swim.

Bearing in mind the provisions of the Mental Health Act, describe in a few words what actions you would take.

The officer thought for a moment, picked up his pen, and wrote: "I would take off my uniform and mingle with the crowd."

We can sympathize with his answer. As a Christian, it is often easier to take off our Christian uniforms and mingle with the crowd. But we are called to remain distinctive, to retain our Christian identity, wherever we are and whatever the circumstances.

A Christian is called to be a chrysalis rather than a chameleon. A chrysalis turns into a beautiful butterfly. A chameleon has the power to change color: many can assume shades of green, yellow, cream or dark brown. It is popularly thought to change color to match its background. Similarly, chameleon Christians merge with their surroundings, happy to be Christians in the company of other Christians, but willing to change their standards in an environment that is not Christian. Legend has it that an experiment was carried out on a chameleon. It was put on a tartan plaid background, could not take the tension, and exploded! The chameleon Christian experiences an almost unbearable tension in his or her life and, unlike the chrysalis Christian, does not reach his or her potential.

Christians are not called to fit in with their background, but to be different. Being different does not mean being odd. We are not called to wear weird clothes or to start speaking in a peculiar religious language. We can be normal! The abnormality that some people feel to be a necessary part of Christianity is complete nonsense. Indeed, a relationship with God through Jesus should bring integration to our personalities. The more like Jesus we become, the more "normal" we become—in the sense that we become more fully human.

When we follow Christ, we are free to shed patterns and habits that bring us and others down. For example, it means that we should no longer indulge in character assassination behind people's backs. It means we can no longer spend our time grumbling and complaining (if that is what we were like before). It means that we can no longer conform to the world's standards of sexual morality. This might all sound very negative, but it should not be so. Rather than

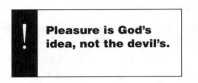

Pleasure is God's idea, not the devil's.

being backbiters, we should be encouragers, constantly looking to build others up out of love for them. Rather than grumbling and complaining, we should be full of thankfulness and joy. Rather than indulging in sexual immorality, we should be demonstrating the blessing of keeping God's standards.

This latter example is one area where Christians are called to be different, but which many find difficult. In my experience of speaking about the Christian faith there is one subject that arises time and time again—the whole question of sexual morality. Questions most frequently asked in this area are, "What about sex outside marriage? Is it wrong? Where does it say so in the Bible? Why is it wrong?"

God's pattern here, as elsewhere, is far superior to any other. God invented marriage. He also invented sex. He is not, as some seem to think, looking down in astonishment and saying, "Oh my goodness, whatever will they think of next?" C. S. Lewis pointed out that pleasure is God's idea, not the devil's. The Bible affirms our sexuality. God made us sexual beings and designed our sexual organs for our enjoyment. The Bible celebrates sexual intimacy. In the Song of Solomon we see the delight, contentment, and satisfaction it brings.

The inventor of sex also tells us how it can be enjoyed to the full. The biblical context of sexual intercourse is the lifelong commitment in marriage between one man and one woman. The Christian doctrine is set out in Genesis 2:24 and quoted by Jesus in Mark 10:7: "For this reason a man will leave his father and mother and be united to his wife, and the two will become one flesh." Marriage involves the public act of leaving parents and making a lifelong commitment.

It involves being united with one's partner—the Hebrew word meaning literally "glued together"—not just physically and biologically, but emotionally, psychologically, spiritually, and socially. This is the Christian context of "one flesh" The biblical doctrine of marriage is the most exciting, thrilling, and positive view of marriage that exists. It sets before us God's perfect plan.

God warns of the danger of going outside the boundaries He has laid down. There is no such thing as "casual sex." Every act of sexual intercourse effects a "one flesh" union (1 Corinthians 6:13-20). When this union is broken, people get hurt. If you glue two pieces of cardboard together and then pull them apart, you can hear the sound of ripping and see that bits of each are left behind on the other. Similarly, becoming one flesh and then being torn apart leaves scars. We leave broken bits of ourselves in broken relationships. All around us we see what happens when

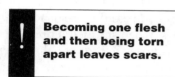

Becoming one flesh and then being torn apart leaves scars.

God's standards are ignored. We see broken marriages, broken hearts, hurt children, sexual disease, and messed up lives. On the other hand, in so many Christian marriages where God's standards are kept, we see the blessing that God intended to bestow on the whole area of sex and marriage. Of course, it is never too late. God's love through Jesus can bring forgiveness, heal scars, and restore wholeness to lives that have been torn apart. But it is far better to avoid the necessity of such measures.

So, let us not allow the world to squeeze us into its mold. Let us show the world something far, far better. When light shines, people will be attracted to its glow.

Make a new start

Paul says we are to "be transformed" (Romans 12:2). In other words, be like the chrysalis that changes into a beautiful butterfly. Many are sometimes fearful of change in their life: two caterpillars sitting on a leaf saw a butterfly passing by. One turned to the other and said, "You won't catch me going up in one of those!" Such is our fear of leaving behind what we know.

God does not ask us to leave behind anything that is good. But He does ask us to get rid of the rubbish. Until we leave the rubbish behind we cannot enjoy the wonderful things God has for us. A woman lived on the streets and walked around our church neighborhood. She would ask for money and react

> **God does not ask us to leave behind anything that is good.**

aggressively to those who refused. She walked the streets for years, accompanied by a mass of plastic bags. When she died, I presided at the funeral. Although I didn't expect anyone to be there, there were in fact several well-dressed people at the service. I discovered afterwards that this woman had inherited a large fortune. She had acquired a luxurious flat and many valuable paintings, but she chose to live on the streets with her plastic bags full of rubbish. She could not bring herself to leave her lifestyle, and she never enjoyed her inheritance.

As Christians we have inherited far more—all the riches of Christ. In order to enjoy these treasures, we have to leave behind the rubbish in our lives. Paul tells us to "hate what is evil" (Romans 12:9). That is what must be left behind.

Sincere love (vs. 9). In the verses that follow (Romans 12:9-21) we get a glimpse of some of those treasures to be enjoyed:

> Love must be sincere. Hate what is evil; cling to what is good. Be devoted to one another in brotherly love. Honor one another above yourselves. Never be lacking in zeal, but keep your spiritual

fervor, serving the Lord. Be joyful in hope, patient in affliction, faithful in prayer. Share with God's people who are in need. Practice hospitality.

Bless those who persecute you; bless and do not curse. Rejoice with those who rejoice; mourn with those who mourn. Live in harmony with one another. Do not be proud, but be willing to associate with people of low position. Do not be conceited.

Do not repay anyone evil for evil. Be careful to do what is right in the eyes of everybody. If it is possible, as far as it depends on you, live at peace with everyone. Do not take revenge, my friends, but leave room for God's wrath, for it is written: "It is mine to avenge; I will repay," says the Lord. On the contrary: "If your enemy is hungry, feed him; if he is thirsty, give him something to drink. In doing this, you will heap burning coals on his head." Do not be overcome by evil, but overcome evil with good.

The Greek word for "sincere" means "without hypocrisy," or literally "without play acting" or "without a mask." We all put up fronts to protect ourselves. I certainly did before I was a Christian (and it carried on to some extent afterwards—though it shouldn't have). I said, in effect, "I don't really like what I am inside, so I will pretend I am somebody different."

If other people are doing the same then there are two masks meeting. The real people never meet. This is the opposite of sincere love. Sincere love means dropping the fronts and taking the risk of revealing ourselves. When we know that God loves us as we are, we are set free to take off our masks. This means that there is a completely new depth in our relationships.

Enthusiasm for the Lord (vs. 11). Sometimes people are cynical about enthusiasm, but there is nothing wrong with it. There is a joy and excitement, a spiritual fervor (vs. 11) that comes from our relationship with God. This initial experience of Christ is meant to last, and not to peter out. Paul says, "Never be lacking in zeal, but keep your spiritual fervor, serving the Lord." The longer we have been Christians, the more enthusiastic we should be.

Harmonious relationships (vss. 13-21). Paul urges Christians to live in harmony with one another and to be generous (vs. 13), hospitable (vs. 13), forgiving (vs. 14), empathetic (vs. 15), and to live at peace with everyone (vs. 18). This is a glorious picture of the Christian family into which God calls us, beckoning us into an atmosphere of love, joy, patience, faithfulness, generosity, hospitality, blessing, rejoicing, harmony, humility, and peace; where good is not overcome by evil, but evil is overcome by good. These are some of the treasures in store when we leave behind the rubbish.

How do we do it?

Present your bodies

This requires an act of the will. Paul commands us, in view of everything that God has done for us, to offer our bodies "as living sacrifices, holy and pleasing to God" (Romans 12:1). God wants us to offer all of ourselves and all of our lives.

Time. We offer our time, our most valuable possession. We need to give Him all our time. This does not mean we spend all of it in prayer and Bible study, but that we allow His priorities to be established in us.

It is easy to get our priorities wrong. An advertisement appeared in a newspaper: "Farmer seeks lady with tractor with view to companionship and possible marriage. Please send picture of tractor." I don't think the farmer had his priorities quite right. Our priorities must be our relationships, and our number one priority is our relationship with God. We need to set aside time to be alone with Him.

We also need to set aside time to be with other Christians—on Sundays and perhaps some mid-week meeting where we can encourage one another.

Ambitions. Secondly, we need to offer our ambitions to the Lord, saying to Him, "Lord, I trust you with my ambitions and hand them over to you." He asks us to seek His kingdom and His righteousness as our foremost ambition, and then He promises to meet all our other needs (Matthew 6:33). This does not necessarily mean our former ambitions disappear; they may become secondary to Christ's ambitions for us. For instance, there is nothing wrong with wanting to be successful in our jobs, provided that our motivation in everything is seeking His kingdom and His righteousness, and that we use what we have for His glory.

Possessions. Thirdly, we need to offer God our possessions and our money. The New Testament does not ban private property or making money or saving or even enjoying the good things of life. What is forbidden is a selfish accumulation for ourselves, an unhealthy obsession with material things, and putting our trust in riches. What promises security leads to perpetual insecurity and leads us away from God (Matthew 7:9-24). Generous giving is the appropriate response to the generosity of God and the needs of others around us. It is also the best way to break the hold of materialism in our lives.

Ears and eyes, mouths and hands. Next, we need to give Him our ears (that is, what we listen to). We must be prepared to stop listening to gossip and other things that drag us and others down. Instead we need to attune our ears to hearing what God says through the Bible, through prayer, and through books and tapes and so on. We offer Him our eyes and what we see. Again, some things we look at can harm us through jealousy, lust, or some other sin. Other things can lead us closer to God. Rather than criticizing the people we meet, we should see them through God's eyes and ask, "How can I be a blessing to that person?"

Then we need to give Him our mouths. The apostle James reminds us what a powerful instrument the tongue is (James 3:1-12).

We have to be prepared to go God's way and not ours.

We can use our tongues to destroy, to deceive, to curse, to gossip, or to draw attention to ourselves. Or we can use our tongues to worship God and to encourage others. Further, we offer Him our hands. We can use our hands either to take for ourselves or to give to others in practical acts of service. Finally, we offer Him our sexuality. We can either use our sexuality for our own self-gratification or we can reserve it for the good and pleasure of our marriage partner.

We cannot pick and choose. Paul says, "Offer your bodies"—that is, every part of us. The extraordinary paradox is that as we give Him everything we find freedom. Living for ourselves is slavery; but "His service is perfect freedom," as the *Book of Common Prayer* puts it.

As living sacrifices

Doing all this may involve some sacrifice. As William Barclay put it, "Jesus came not to make life easy but to make men great." We have to be prepared to go God's way and not ours. We have to be willing to give up anything in our lives that we know is wrong and put things right where restitution is required. We need to be willing to fly His flag in a world that may be hostile to the Christian faith.

In many parts of the world, being a Christian involves physical persecution. More Christians have died for their faith in this century than in any other. Others are imprisoned and tortured. We, in the free world, are privileged to live in a society where Christians are not persecuted. The criticism and mocking we may receive are hardly worth mentioning compared to the suffering of the early church and the persecuted church today.

Nevertheless, our faith may involve making sacrifices. For example, I have a friend who was disinherited by his parents when he became a Christian. I know one couple who had to sell their home because they felt that as Christians they must let the government know that over the years they had not been entirely honest in their tax returns.

I had a great friend who was sleeping with his girlfriend before he became a Christian. When he began to look at the Christian faith, he realized that this would have to change if he put his faith in Christ. For many months he wrestled with it. Eventually both he and his girlfriend became Christians and decided that from that moment they would stop sleeping together. For various reasons, they were not in a position to get married for another two-and-a-half years. There was a sacrifice involved for them, although they do not see it in that way. God has blessed them richly with a happy marriage and four wonderful children. But at the time there was a cost involved.

WHY SHOULD WE DO IT?

What God has planned for our future

God loves us and wants the very best for our lives. He wants us to entrust our lives to Him so that we can "test and approve what God's will is—his good, pleasing and perfect will" (Romans 12:2).

I sometimes think that the chief work of the devil is to give people a false view of God. The Hebrew word for "Satan" means "slanderer." He slanders God, telling us that God is not to be trusted. He tells us God is a spoilsport and that God wants to ruin our lives.

Often we believe these lies. We think that if we trust our Father in heaven with our lives, He will take away all our enjoyment in life.

Imagine a human father like that. Suppose one of my sons were to come to me and say, "Daddy, I want to give you my day to spend it however you want." Of course, I would not say, "Right, that is what I have been waiting for. You can spend the day locked in the closet!"

It is absurd to consider that God would treat us worse than a human father. He loves us more than any human father and wants the very best for our lives. His will for us is good. He wants the very best (as every good father does). It is pleasing—it will please Him and us in the long run. It is perfect—we will not be able to improve on it.

He loves us more than any human father and wants the very best for us.

Sadly, people feel they can improve on it. They think, "I can do a little better than God. God is a bit out of touch. He hasn't caught up with the modern world and the things that we enjoy. I think I will run my own life and keep God well out of it." But we can never do a better job than God, and sometimes we end up making an awful mess.

One of my sons was given some homework that involved making an advertisement for a Roman slave market. He spent most of the weekend doing it. When he had finished the drawing and written all the inscriptions, he wanted to make it look two thousand years old. The way to do that, he had been told, is to hold the paper over a flame until it turns brown, which gives it the appearance of age. This is quite a tricky job for a nine-year-old, so my wife, Pippa, offered to help—several times—but could not persuade him. He insisted on doing it himself. The result was that the advertisement was burned to a cinder, accompanied by many tears of frustration and hurt pride.

Some people insist on running their own lives. They do not want any help, they will not trust God, and often they end up in tears. But God gives us a second chance. My son did his poster again, and this time he trusted Pippa to do the delicate singeing operation. If we will trust God with our lives, then He will show us what His will is—His good, pleasing, and perfect will."

What God has done for us

The little sacrifices God asks us to make are nothing when we compare them with the sacrifice that God made for us. C. T. Studd, the nineteenth-century England cricket captain who gave up wealth and comfort (and cricket!) to serve God in inland China, once said, "If Jesus Christ be God, and he died for me, nothing is too hard for me to do for him." C. T. Studd was looking to Jesus. The writer of Hebrews urges us, "Let us run with perseverance the race that is set

before us, looking to Jesus the pioneer and perfecter of our faith, who for the joy that was set before him endured the cross, despising the shame, and is seated at the right hand of the throne of God" (Hebrews 12:1, 2, *Revised Standard Version*).

As we look at Jesus, God's only Son who "endured the cross," we see how much God loves us. It is absurd not to trust Him. If God loves us so much we can be sure He will not deprive us of anything good. Paul wrote, "He who did not spare his own Son, but gave him up for us all—how will he not also, along with him, graciously give us all things?" (Romans 8:32). Our motivation for living the Christian life is the love of the Father. Our model in life is the example of the Son. The means by which we can live this life is the power of the Holy Spirit.

How great God is and what a privilege it is to walk in a relationship with Him, to be loved by Him, and to serve Him, all our lives. It is the best, most rewarding, fulfilling, meaningful, satisfying way to live. Indeed it is here we find the answers to the great questions of life.

Notes

1. Ronald Brown (ed.), *Bishop's Brew* (Arthur James Ltd., 1989).

2. By kind permission of Bernard Levin.

3. *Ibid.*

4. C. S. Lewis, *Timeless at Heart*, Christian Apologetics (Fount).

5. C. S. Lewis, *Surprised by Joy* (Fontana, 1955).

6. Bishop Michael Marshall, *Church of England Newspaper*, August 9, 1991.

7. John Martyn, *Church of England Newspaper*, November 2, 1990.

8. Josephus, Antiquities, XVIII 63f. Some suggest that the text has been corrupted; nonetheless, the evidence of Josephus confirms the historical existence of Jesus.

9. F. J. A. Hort, *The New Testament in the Original Greek*, Vol. I, page 561 (New York: Macmillan Co.).

10. Sir Frederic Kenyon, *The Bible and Archaeology* (Harper and Row, 1940).

11. If you are interested in pursuing the subject of Gospel historicity, I would recommend reading R. T. France, *The Evidence for Jesus* from The Jesus Library (Hodder & Stoughton, 1986) or N.T. Wright, *Jesus and the Victory of God (SPCK,1996).*

12. C. S. Lewis, *Mere Christianity* (Fount, 1952).

13. *Ibid.*

14. Bernard Ramm, *Protestant Christian Evidence* (Moody Press).

15. By kind permission of Bernard Levin.

16. Lord Hailsham, *The Door Wherein I Went* (Fount/Collins, 1975).

17. Wilbur Smith, *The Incomparable Book* (Beacon Publications, 1961).

18. Josh McDowell, *The Resurrection Factor* (Thomas Nelson, 1992).

19. Michael Green, *Evangelism through the Local Church* (Hodder & Stoughton, 1990).

20. Michael Green, *Man Alive* (InterVarsity Press, 1968).

21. C. S. Lewis, *Surprised by Joy* (Fontana, 1955).

22. Bishop J. C. Ryle, *Expository Thoughts on The Gospel*, Vol. III, John 1:1–John 10:30 (Evangelical Press, 1977).

23. *The Journal of the Lawyers' Christian Fellowship.*

24. John Wimber, *Equipping the Saints* Vol. 2, No. 2, Spring 1988 (Vineyard Ministries Int.).

25. Lesslie Newbigin, *Foolishness to the Greeks* (SPCK, 1995).

26. C. S. Lewis, *The Last Battle* (HarperCollins, 1956).

27. John W. Wenham, *Christ and the Bible* (Tyndale: USA, 1972).

28. John Pollock, *Billy Graham: the Authorized Biography* (Hodder & Stoughton, 1966).

29. Bishop Stephen Neill, *The Supremacy of Jesus* (Hodder & Stoughton, 1984).

30. *Family Magazine.*

31. John Stott, *Christian Counter-Culture* (InterVarsity Press, 1978).

32. Quoted in John Stott, *Christian Counter-Culture* (InterVarsity Press, 1978).

33. Michael Bordeaux, *Risen Indeed* (Dartman, Longmon Todd, 1983)

34. John Eddison, *A Study in Spiritual Power* (Highland, 1982).

35. *Ibid.*

36. F. W. Bourne, *Billy Bray: The King's Son* (Epworth Press, 1937).

37. J. Hopkins and H. Richardson (eds.), *Anselm of Canterbury, Proslogion Vol 1* (SCM Press, 1974).

38. Malcolm Muggeridge, *Conversion* (Collins, 1988).

39. Richard Wurmbrand, *In God's Underground* (Living Sacrifice Books, 1973).

40. Eddie Gibbs, *I Believe In Church Growth* (Hodder & Stoughton).

41. David Watson, *One In The Spirit*, (Hodder & Stoughton).

42. Murray Watts, *Rolling in the Aisles* (Monarch Publications, 1987).

43. There has been a great deal of discussion in recent years about whether this experience of the Holy Spirit should be described as "baptism," "filling," "releasing," "empowering," or by some other term. For all that has been said and written on the subject, I do not think it is entirely clear from the New Testament which is the right term. What is clear is that we need the experience of the power of the Holy Spirit in our lives. I myself think that the filling of the Holy Spirit is the most faithful to the New Testament, and I have used that expression in this chapter.

44. Martyn Lloyd-Jones, *Romans*, Vol. VIII (Banner of Truth, 1974).

45. Wimber & Springer (editors), *Riding the Third Wave* (Marshall Pickering).

46. Alan MacDonald, *Films in Close Up*, (Frameworks, 1991).

47. Michael Green, *I Believe in Satan's Downfall* (Hodder & Stoughton, 1981).

48. Jean-Baptiste Vianney.

49. C. S. Lewis, *The Screwtape Letters* (Fount, 1942).

50. C. S. Lewis, *The Great Divorce* (Fount, 1973).

51. J. C. Pollock, *Hudson Taylor and Maria* (Hodder & Stoughton, 1962).

52. Irenaeus, *Against Heresies*, II Ch. XXXII.

53. David Watson, *I Believe in the Church* (Hodder & Stoughton, 1978).

54. C. S. Lewis, *Fern Seeds and Elephants* (Fontana, 1975).

Study Guide

BY DAVID STONE

The aim of the questions that follow is to help you get to the heart of what Nicky Gumbel has written and challenge you to apply what you learn to your own life. The questions can be used by individuals or by small groups meeting together.

Chapter 1: Christianity: Boring, Untrue, and Irrelevant?

1. Why do you think people today tend to regard Christianity as boring, untrue, and irrelevant (p. 11 and following)?
2. "Life without a relationship with God through Jesus Christ is like a television without the antenna" (pp. 15, 16). How do you react to this statement? Why?
3. What possible critical responses to Christianity does Nicky identify here (p. 16 and following)? How might these be answered?
4. Nicky makes a sharp distinction between the intellectual acceptance of truth on the one hand and experiencing it on the other (pp. 17, 18). Why is this so important when thinking about Christianity?
5. What does "eternal life" mean (p. 21)? How can it begin now?

Chapter 2: Who is Jesus?

1. How would you answer someone who suggested that to become a Christian is not a good idea because it involves "a blind leap of faith" (p. 23)?

2. How strong do you think the New Testament evidence about Jesus is (p. 24 and following)? Why?

3. Given that Jesus didn't actually "go around saying the words, 'I am God'" (p. 27), what evidence is there that He is divine?

4. Why is the physical resurrection of Jesus Christ the "cornerstone of Christianity" (p. 36 and following)? What do you make of the evidence for this event?

5. What are the "only three realistic possibilities" about who Jesus is (p. 40)? Which do you think is right? Why?

6. If Jesus is the Son of God, what are the implications for you?

Chapter 3: Why Did Jesus Die?

1. What does the author identify as "the greatest problem that confronts every person" (p. 44)? Do you agree? Why?

2. Why does the New Testament insist that breaking any part of God's law makes us guilty of breaking all of it (p. 45)?

3. What other results of sin does the Bible spell out (p. 45 and following)? To what extent have you experienced these?

4. What has God done about human sin (p. 47 and following)? How do you know (if you do!) that He has dealt with the problems caused by your sin?

5. What does "justification" mean (p. 49 and following)? How does the death of Jesus bring it about for us?

6. What does it mean to be "set free from the power of sin" (pp. 51, 52)? In what ways is it true that "sin's hold over us is broken"?

7. The writer of Hebrews tells us that it is "impossible for the blood of bulls and goats to take away sins." What, then, was the point of the elaborate Old Testament system of sacrifices (p. 52)?

8. How would you answer the suggestion that "God is unjust because He punished Jesus, an innocent party, instead of us" (pp. 52, 53)?

Chapter 4: How Can I Be Sure of My Faith?

1. What does the idea of a "relationship with God" suggest to you (p. 57 and following)?
2. Why is it so important to be sure of our faith based on the promises of the Bible rather than our own feelings (p. 59)?
3. Which promises does Nicky focus on (p. 60 and following)? Which is the most meaningful for you? Why?
4. What would you say to someone who said that he was trying to live a reasonably good life and hoped that God would therefore let him into heaven when he dies (p. 62 and following)?
5. What was so special about the death of Jesus (p. 63 and following)? What did it achieve? How is this relevant for you?
6. How does the activity of the Holy Spirit help us to be sure of our faith in Christ (p. 64 and following)? To what extent have you noticed this in your own life?
7. "It is not arrogant to be sure" (p. 67). Do you still have doubts that stop you being certain of your faith? In what ways has this chapter helped to deal with those doubts?

Chapter 5: Why and How Should I Read the Bible?

1. What is the main difference between the Bible and other "inspired" works of literature (p. 73)?
2. For Jesus, "what the Scriptures said, God said" (pp. 73, 74). Do you share that belief?
3. Do you have difficulties with the Bible that undermine your ability to trust it as the Word of God? How might these be resolved?
4. How would you answer someone who claimed that using the Bible as a rulebook is unnecessarily restrictive (p. 77 and following)?
5. Nicky says that as well as being a manual, the Bible is also "a love letter" (p. 78). How have you experienced that in your life?

6. What do you expect to happen when you read the Bible (p. 80 and following)?

7. What practical advice would you offer to someone who wants to hear God speak through the Bible (p. 83 and following)?

Chapter 6: Why and How Do I Pray?

1. The author says, "When we pray, the whole Trinity is involved" (p. 88). Explain what he means.

2. Nicky gives various reasons for praying (p. 90 and following). Which of these do you relate to?

3. What answer would you give to those who "have philosophical objections to the concept that prayer can change events" (p. 92)?

4. What are the "good reasons why we may not always get what we ask for" (p. 92 and following)?

5. What major ingredients does prayer need to include (p. 96)?

6. How does the example of Jesus in the Lord's Prayer guide us in our praying (p. 95 and following)?

7. What guidelines should we follow when we pray for our own concerns (p. 98)?

8. Why is prayer "at the heart of Christianity" (p. 101)?

Chapter 7: How Does God Guide Us?

1. What are the things that prevent us from receiving God's guidance for our lives (p. 105 and following)?

2. What are the ways in which God speaks to people today (p. 106 and following)?

3. How can prayer become more of a two-way conversation (p. 108 and following)?

4. What part does common sense play in discovering God's will for our lives (p. 111 and following)?

5. What suggestions would you make to someone looking for a spiritual advisor (p. 113 and following)?

6. What should we do when the answer we need from God takes a long time to come (p. 117 and following)?

7. What should we do if we believe we have "made a mess of our lives" (pp. 117, 118)?

Chapter 8: Who is the Holy Spirit?

1. What parallels are there between the Holy Spirit's activity in the Bible and today (pp. 120, 121)?

2. What is the main difference between what the Holy Spirit does in the Old Testament and what He does in the New Testament and today (p. 125 and following)?

3. The author uses the analogy of a sponge to explain the difference between being "baptized in" and "filled with the Holy Spirit" (p. 128). Can you think of another analogy?

4. What is the result in a person's life when "rivers of living water" flow through them (pp. 128, 129)?

5. What was Peter's explanation of what happened on the Day of Pentecost (pp. 130, 131)?

Chapter 9: What Does the Holy Spirit Do?

1. What happens when someone is "born again" (pp. 133, 134)?

2. What is the primary work of the Holy Spirit in a person before he or she becomes a Christian (p. 134)?

3. How does our status before God change after we become Christians (p. 135 and following)?

4. How does the Holy Spirit help us "to develop our relationship with God" (p. 139 and following)?

5. In what ways does the Holy Spirit make us more like Jesus (p. 141 and following)?

6. What would you suggest Christians can do to "keep the unity of the Spirit" (pp. 143, 144)?

7. What does the author identify as "one of the major problems in

the church at large" (pp. 145, 146)? What can be done about it?

8. The author says that although every Christian is indwelt by the Holy Spirit, not every Christian is filled with the Spirit (pp. 147, 148). What advice would you give to someone who wanted to bridge that gap?

Chapter 10: How Can I Be Filled With the Spirit?

1. "In an ideal world every Christian would be filled with the Holy Spirit from the moment of conversion" (p. 149 and following). Why do you think this doesn't always happen?

2. How important do you think are experiences of the power of the Holy Spirit (p. 151 and following)?

3. Why is the appropriate expression of emotion in our relationship with God so important (p. 153 and following)? How does this differ from emotionalism?

4. What exactly is the gift of tongues for (p. 156 and following)?

5. How would you answer someone who suggested that Christians who don't have the gift of tongues are missing out on something essential (p. 158 and following)?

Chapter 11: How Can I Resist Evil?

1. Why do you think "many Westerners find belief in the devil more difficult than belief in God" (p. 165)?

2. What dangers are there in "an excessive and unhealthy interest" in the devil (pp. 168, 169)?

3. What tactics does the devil use in an individual's life (p. 169 and following)?

4. What is the difference between temptation to sin and sin itself (p. 173 and following)? Why is this distinction so important?

5. How does our relationship to the devil change when we become Christians (p. 173 and following)? What are the practical consequences of this?

6. In Ephesians 6 Paul mentions six pieces of the Christian's armor. What do you think each of these means in practice?
7. In what ways are we called upon to be involved in the spiritual warfare between good and evil (p. 178, 179)?

Chapter 12: Why and How Should We Tell Others?

1. What answer would you give to someone who says that Christianity is "a private matter" (p. 181 and following)?
2. What are the "two opposite dangers" in telling people about Christ that the author describes (p. 183 and following)?
3. What does it mean in practice to be salt and light to those around us (p. 185 and following)?
4. How can we be better equipped to answer the objections that people may have to the Christian faith (p. 188 and following)?
5. What are some ways that you could bring people to Jesus?
6. Prayer is essential in the area of telling others the Good News (p. 194 and following). Why?
7. How should we respond when we get negative reactions to speaking about Jesus (pp. 195, 196)?

Chapter 13: Does God Heal Today?

1. What would you say to someone who shows fear and skepticism over the question of healing (p. 200)?
2. What does the author mean by the "now" and "not yet" of the kingdom of God (p. 203 and following)? How can understanding this help us in thinking about healing?
3. How would you answer someone who claimed that Jesus' command to His disciples that they should heal the sick no longer applies to us today (p. 205 and following)?
4. "Not everyone we pray for will necessarily be healed" (p. 211). Why not? Does this matter?

5. Why is it important to "pray with simplicity" (p. 212)? What are the practical steps that the author recommends (pp. 212, 213)?

6. What would you say to someone who thought that healing had not taken place because the person concerned did not have enough faith (p. 213)?

7. Why is it important to persist in praying for healing, even when "we do not see immediate, dramatic results" (p. 213 and following)?

Chapter 14: What About the Church?

1. What definition would you give to the word "church"?

2. How does the Greek word for church help to explain what it is all about (p. 219)?

3. What are the three types of Christian gathering referred to in the New Testament (p. 220 and following)?

4. "The church is one, even though it often appears divided" (p. 221 and following). What can we do about the things that divide us?

5. "… we cannot be a Christian alone" (p. 223). Do you agree? Why or why not?

6. What exactly do you need your fellow Christians for (p. 224 and following)? In what ways do they need you?

7. What does "the priesthood of all believers" mean (pp. 227, 228)?

8. In what ways do you think the church falls short of the pattern described in the New Testament (p. 229 and following)? What might we do to change things for the better?

Chapter 15: How Can I Make the Most of the Rest of My Life?

1. In what ways does the world try and squeeze you into its mold (p. 233)? How can you resist this pressure?

2. "The biblical context of sexual intercourse is the lifelong commitment in marriage between one man and one woman" (p. 236). What danger is there in going outside these boundaries?

3. What would you say to someone who has crossed these boundaries and now bitterly regrets what he or she has done (p. 237)?

4. "Until we leave the rubbish behind we cannot enjoy the wonderful things God has for us" (p. 238). What do you think this means in practice?

5. How can we find out what are God's priorities for our life? (p. 240 and following)?

6. In what ways have you experienced the truth that "our faith may involve making sacrifices" (p. 243)? Was it worth it?

7. "God loves us and wants the very best for our lives" (p. 243). Why is it sometimes difficult to believe this?

8. What does it mean in practice to "look at Jesus" (p. 245)? How does this help in living the Christian life?

Alpha Resources

This book is an *Alpha* resource. The *Alpha Course* is a practical introduction to the Christian faith developed by Holy Trinity Brompton
Church in London, England. *Alpha Courses* are now being run
worldwide.

Resources needed for setting up, promoting, and training for the
Alpha Course

- The *Alpha Course* Introductory Video
- *Alpha* Conference Audio Tapes –OR–
- How to Run *Alpha* Video (Volumes 1 and 2)
- *Alpha* Leader's Training Tapes or Videos (set of 3 talks)
- The *Alpha Course* Leader's Guide (one for each small-group
leader and helper)
- How to Run the *Alpha Course:* A Handbook for Directors,
Leaders, and Helpers

Resources needed for running the *Alpha Course*

- The *Alpha Course* Tapes –OR–
- The *Alpha Course* Videos (5-video set including 15 talks)
- How to Run the *Alpha Course:* A Handbook for Directors,
Leaders, and Helpers
- The *Alpha Course* Manual (one for each small-group
participant and leader)

- The *Alpha Course* Leader's Guide (one for each small-group leader and helper)
- Registration Brochures (one for each potential participant; sold in packets of 50)
- *Why Jesus?* (recommended reading for each participant)
- *Questions of Life* (recommended reading for each leader and participant)
- *Searching Issues* (recommended reading for each leader and participant)

In North America, all *Alpha* resources are published by Cook Ministry Resources, a division of Cook Communications Ministries.

In the USA, call or write:

> Cook Ministry Resources
> 4050 Lee Vance View
> Colorado Springs, CO 80918-7100
> 1-800-36-ALPHA (1-800-362-5742)

In Canada, call or write:

> Beacon Distributing
> P.O. Box 98
> 55 Woodslee Ave.
> Paris Ontario N3L 3E5
> 1-800-263-2664

Alpha Books

BY **NICKY GUMBEL**

Why Jesus?
A booklet recommended for all participants at the start of the *Alpha Course.*

Why Christmas?
The Christmas version of *Why Jesus?*

Questions of Life
The *Alpha Course* in book form. In fifteen compelling chapters the author points the way to an authentic Christianity which is exciting and relevant to today's world.

Searching Issues
The seven issues most often raised by participants of the *Alpha Course:* suffering, other religions, sex before marriage, the New Age, homosexuality, science and Christianity, and the Trinity.

A Life Worth Living
What happens after *Alpha?* Based on the book of Philippians, this is an invaluable next step for those who have just completed the *Alpha Course,* and for anyone eager to put their faith on a firm biblical footing.

Challenging Lifestyle
An in-depth look at the Sermon on the Mount (Matthew 5—7). The author shows that Jesus' teaching flies in the face of modern lifestyle and presents us with a radical alternative.

Telling Others
This book includes the principles and practicalities of setting up and running an *Alpha Course*. It also includes personal accounts of lives changed while attending an *Alpha Course*.

The Heart of Revival
Ten studies based on Isaiah 40—66, drawing out important truths for today. This course seeks to understand what revival might mean and how we can prepare to be part of it.

30 Days
Follow Nicky through 30 days of focused Bible reading and prayer to see how God's Word and His Spirit can change your life. Start a new habit that will give life and energy to everyday!

To order, call 1-800-36-ALPHA

Or visit your local Christian Bookstore